"Stephen Olford has not only spent his life preaching beautiful expository sermons, he is a peerless teacher of preachers. The Stephen F. Olford Biblical Preaching Library provides substantive examples on how to do it. It will be a great help to many preachers."

Dr. R. Kent Hughes, Senior Pastor
College Church, Wheaton, Illinois

"Stephen Olford is a master expositor and genius at outline clarity. . . . Most preachers can neither walk across the street or travel across the continent to hear him. But they can glean the treasures of his preaching life from The Stephen F. Olford Biblical Preaching Library. I heartily commend this resource."

Dr. Maxie E. Dunham, Senior Pastor
Christ United Methodist Church, Memphis, Tennessee

"Every informed preacher of the Word of God knows of the spiritual power, impeccable scholarship, and practicality of the materials produced by Stephen Olford. Without reservation, I commend The Stephen F. Olford Biblical Preaching Library."

Dr. Adrian Rogers, Senior Pastor
Bellevue Baptist Church, Cordova, Tennessee

Books in the Stephen F. Olford Biblical Preaching Library

Living Words and Loving Deeds

*Messages on Christ's Claims
and Miracles in the
Gospel of John*

Stephen F. Olford

BAKER BOOK HOUSE
Grand Rapids, Michigan 49516

ISBN: 0-8010-6721-9

These resources were adapted from material published by the Institute for
Biblical Preaching, Box 757800, Memphis, TN 38175-7800.

The King James Version is used as the basis for this Bible study. Other
versions occasionally used are the New King James Version (NKJV) and the
Revised Version (RV).

The author is grateful to the many copyright owners for the use of their
material.

Contents

Introduction

As you preach these expository sermons, I want to emphasize the need for the *application* of truth to your hearers. No one has put this more succinctly and ably than Rev. John R. W. Stott. He writes: "Exposition is not a synonym for exegesis. True biblical preaching goes beyond the elucidation of the text to its application. Indeed, the discipline of discovering a text's original meaning is of little profit if we do not go on to discern its contemporary message. We have to ask of every Scripture not only 'what did it mean?' but 'what does it say?' Perhaps it is the failure to ask both these questions, and to persevere with the asking until the answers come, which is the greatest tragedy of current preaching. We evangelicals enjoy studying the text with a view to opening it up, but we are often weak in applying it to the realities of modern life. Our liberal colleagues, however, tend to make the opposite mistake. Their great concern is to relate to the modern world, but their message is less than fully biblical. Thus almost nobody is building bridges between the biblical world and the modern world, across the wide chasm of 2,000 years of changing culture. Yet preaching is essentially a bridge-building exercise. It is the exacting task of relating God's Word to our world with an equal degree of faithfulness and relevance.

"If we are to build bridges for the Word of God to penetrate the real world, we have to take seriously both the biblical text and the contemporary scene, and study both. We cannot afford to remain on either side of the cultural divide. To withdraw from the world into the Bible (which is escapism) or from the Bible into the world (which is conformity), will be fatal to our preaching ministry. Either mistake makes bridge building impossible and noncommunication inevitable. On the one hand, we preachers need to be as familiar with the Bible 'as the housewife with her needle, the merchant with his ledger, the mariner with his ship' (Spurgeon). On the other, we have to grapple with the much more difficult—and usually less congenial—task of studying the modern world. We have to look and listen and read and watch television. We have to go to the theater and the movies (though selectively), because nothing mirrors contemporary society more faithfully than the stage and the screen.

"It has been a great help to me to have the stimulus of a reading group. Its members are intelligent young graduates (doctors, lawyers, teachers, architects, and others). We meet monthly when I am in London, having previously agreed to read the same book or see the same play or movie. Then we spend a whole evening together, share our reactions, and seek to develop a Christian response.

"As the nineteenth-century German theologian Tholuck said, 'a sermon ought to have heaven for its father and the earth for its mother.' But if such sermons are to be born, heaven and earth have to meet in the preacher."[1]

With the foregoing in mind, I enthusiastically commend to you the outlines in this book. The studies in John's Gospel are under the general subject of *God Alive.* Seven sermons will be on God Alive in Living Discourses and another seven on God Alive in Living Miracles. In these two series of "sevens" we have the two aspects of John's portrait of the Son of God. In the seven "I am's" we have a revelation of his *person;* in the seven "signs" we have the revelation of his *power.* What a Christ we have to preach! Is it any wonder that Paul, in his ministry, determined to "preach Christ crucified, to the Jews a stumbling block and to the Greeks foolishness, but to those who are called, both Jews and Greeks, Christ the power of God and the wisdom of God" (1 Cor. 1:23–24).

May I remind you that these are not "canned sermons," but rather resource materials for adaptation and application to your own style of expository preaching. So I exhort you, "Preach the word. . . . Do the work of an evangelist, fulfill your ministry" (2 Tim. 4:2, 5).

Stephen F. Olford

Part 1

God Alive in Discourses from the Gospel of John

1

The Bread of Life

6:29-36, 47-58

"I am the bread of life" (6:35).

Introduction

In the East, bread was the staple of life, or the principal food of the people. All other dishes were considered as accessories. Therefore, bread had a sacredness all its own. Even today, if you go to the East you will find that Jews or Arabs never tread a piece of bread under foot. However soiled or contaminated it might be, they never despise nor disregard it. An Arab walking down a village street and seeing a piece of bread on the ground would be careful to pick it up and put it in a niche in the wall, ready for some hungry beggar or dog.

This view of the importance and sanctity of bread is expressed over and over again in the Bible, so that the words of our Savior carry an even greater significance when interpreted by the rest of Scripture. Needless to say, the bread of which our Lord was speaking, in the passage before us, was not the material bread which satisfies physical hunger, but the heavenly bread which satisfies the spiritual hunger of man. And just as the material bread is fundamental to man's physical life, so the heavenly bread is essential to man's spiritual life.

I. Heavenly Bread Supplies Spiritual Life

"I am the living bread which came down from heaven: if any man eat of this bread, he shall live for ever" (6:51). In order to become the Bread of Life to men and women who were spiritually dead:

A. Christ Was Bruised for Us

He was the "bread corn . . . bruised" (Isa. 28:28). Before bread can be made, corn has to be crushed under the grindstone, and then mixed in the kneading trough.

This is a truly vivid picture of the suffering through which our Lord had to go, before he could provide spiritual nutrition for you and me. Isaiah tells us that "He was wounded for our transgressions, he was bruised for our iniquities" (Isa. 53:5).

Illustration

An infidel fireman once rescued a little boy from a burning cottage. To do so he had to climb a hot piping, and his hands were badly scarred. The woman who cared for the boy perished in the fire. The question arose as to who would take the boy. A couple came forward, saying, "We should like to have him; we have plenty of money and no children of our own; we would give him a good education and a good start in life." Others offered the boy a home. Then the fireman spoke up: "I should like to have him," and he showed his scarred hands. All agreed that he had the greatest claim to the child. Some objected, knowing the man was an unbeliever. However, the boy was adopted by the fireman who proved a good father to him and loved him as his own child. One day he took him to an art gallery. The boy caught sight of a painting of Christ on the cross, and asked the man, "Who was that, daddy?" The man tried to silence the boy, and quickly drew him away from the picture, which so impressed the child who gave him no peace till he had heard the gospel story. As the man was saying that Jesus let them put Him on the cross for our sins, the truth shone into his heart, and he believed and yielded himself to the One who has the greatest claim on each one of us.[1]

B. Christ Was Baked for Us

He was the "meal offering [baked] . . . in the oven" (Lev. 2:4, RV). What transpired in the darkness of that oven of God's holy wrath will never be understood by finite minds. All we know is that it was in the heat of that indescribable experience that the Son of God cried out, "My God, my God, why hast thou forsaken me?"

Illustration

Yet once Immanuel's orphaned cry the universe
   hath shaken:
It went up single, echoless, "My God, I am forsaken!"
It went up from His holy lips amid His lost creation
That no one else need ever cry that cry of desolation.[2]

Amplification

Amplify the symbolic meaning of the meal offering: "(1) Fine flour speaks of the evenness and balance of the character of Christ, of that perfection in which no quality was in excess, none lacking; (2) fire, of his testing by suffering, even unto death; (3) frankincense, of the fragrance of His life before God (see Exod. 30:34, note); (4) absence of leaven, of His character as 'the Truth' (John 14:6, cf. Ex. 12:8, marg.); (5) absence of honey—His was not that mere natural sweetness which may exist quite apart from grace; (6) oil mingled, of Christ as born of the Holy Spirit (Matt. 1:18-23); (7) oil upon, of Christ as baptized with the Spirit (John 1:32; 6:27); (8) the oven, of the unseen, suf-

ferings of Christ—His inner agonies (Matt. 27:45-46; Heb.
2:18); (9) the pan, of His more evident sufferings (e.g.,
Matt. 27:27-31); and (10) salt, of the pungency of the
truth of God—that which arrests the action of leaven."[3]

C. Christ Was Broken for Us

Speaking of his death, he could say, through Paul,
"This is my body, which is broken for you" (1 Cor.
11:24).

By being bruised, baked, and broken for us, the Lord
Jesus became the Bread of Life. He could say, "If any
man eat of this bread, he shall live for ever" (6:51). Will
you look up into his face right now and say, "Lord
Jesus, I thank you for being bruised, baked, and broken
for me. I now receive you as the Bread of Life."

Illustration

During a fearful famine in India some years ago a missionary visiting around the villages met a boy who was
nothing but skin and bones. He ordered him to go at once
to the mission compound and ask for food. The boy
pleaded that he would not be admitted to the compound
unless he had some authorization. So the missionary, taking a slip of paper, addressed a note to the storekeeper and
handed it to the boy, saying, "That is my promise of food
for you." Several days later the poor boy was found lying
dead with the piece of paper perforated and tied around
his neck. He had never acted upon the promise, nor appro-
priated what would have been the means of life for him!

How many people are dying around us today, because
they will not act upon God's promise and come and take
the Bread of Life as it is in the Lord Jesus!

II. Heavenly Bread Sustains Spiritual Life

Jesus said, "As the living Father hath sent me, and I
live by the Father; so he that eateth me, even he shall live
by me" (6:57). Now while the supply of life is communi-

cated the moment the sinner appropriates Christ as the Bread of Life, this new life grows and develops only as the believer continues to feed upon Christ. It is interesting to notice that the Lord Jesus intends us to feed on him, even as he fed on the Father. Listen to these words again: "As the living Father hath sent me, and I live by the Father; so he that eateth me, even he shall live by me" (6:57). How did the Lord Jesus live by the Father?

A. By Feeding on the Word of God

When the Lord Jesus answered Satan's attack in the wilderness he revealed the method by which he sustained his spiritual life. Recall his words for a moment: "Man shall not live by bread alone, but by every word that proceedeth out of the mouth of God" (Matt. 4:4). In other words, Jesus was teaching that material bread is not sufficient. Man must feed constantly on the Bread which comes from God, if his spiritual life is to be sustained.

Jeremiah must have known something of this in his experience when he said, "Thy words were found, and I did eat them; and thy word was unto me the joy and rejoicing of mine heart" (Jer. 15:16).

Illustration

In France, there once lived a poor blind girl who obtained the Gospel of Mark in raised letters and learned to read it by the tips of her fingers. By constant reading, these became callous, and her sense of touch diminished until she could not distinguish the characters. One day, she cut the skin from the ends of her fingers to increase their sensitivity, only to destroy it. She felt that she must now give up her beloved Book, and weeping, pressed it to her lips, saying "Farewell, farewell, sweet word of my Heavenly Father!" To her surprise, her lips, more delicate than her fingers, discerned the form of the letters. All night she perused with her lips the Word of God and overflowed with joy at this new acquisition.[4]

B. By Feeding on the Will of God

He could say, "My meat is to do the will of him that sent me" (John 4:34). As he fulfilled the divine will, so his soul was fed by his heavenly Father.

Similarly for us, to fulfill God's will in everything is to prove the sustained and sustaining quality of the Bread of Life.

Amplification

Study carefully the words of John 4:34 in context and explain how Jesus, dealing with the woman of Samaria, was in fact feeding on the will of God.

Illustration

I had rather be in the heart of Africa in the will of God than on the throne of England out of the will of God.[5]

C. By Feeding on the Work of God

Once again, his words were, "My meat is . . . to finish his work" (John 4:34). The Lord Jesus worked to an hourly program. He was never ahead of his time and never behind it. Each day's work was carefully planned and thoroughly done. In fact, on one occasion when his respected mother suggested he perform a miracle before the appointed moment he said, "Mine hour is not yet come" (John 2:4). And as he did each day's work, so he found the very doing of his task for God food for his soul.

Eating of Christ day by day, as the Bread of Life, involves meditation on his Word, dedication to his will, and consecration to his work.

Illustration

Our life's work is a complete whole, yet it is made up of little things, good works. "We are God's workmanship": and the word Paul uses is the Greek word from which we derive the English word "Poem." In her book *Odd Patterns in the Weaving*—Mrs. Sonia E. Howe in her narration mentions something seen when she was still in her teens. A famous Russian academician was working at a mosaic, a copy of an old oil painting which had been in a famous cathedral. He was putting in tiny pieces of marble, one by one, to carry out the beautiful design. Sonia Howe approached him and said, "Is not this fearfully dull, uninteresting work?" "No, not at all," the artist replied, "for, you see, it is work for eternity."[6]

III. Heavenly Bread Satisfies Spiritual Life

"Jesus said unto them, I am the bread of life: he that cometh to me shall never hunger; and he that believeth on me shall never thirst" (6:35). Man's deepest hunger is spiritual. Whether or not he knows it, he hungers for God, he hungers for truth, and he hungers for life. Whatever else he has in the world he will never be satisfied until he finds the answer to this threefold spiritual hunger. Material things can never fill the soul of man—whether things to eat, things to see, things to wear, or things to do. Neither can the human soul be filled with another human soul, for one empty vessel cannot fill another empty vessel. No wonder St. Augustine expressed it, "Thou hast made us for Thyself, and our restless souls can find no rest until they find their rest in Thee." But the glory of the gospel is this, that in Jesus Christ all spiritual hunger can be satisfied. As the Bread from heaven, he satisfies our hunger for God, our hunger for truth, and our hunger for life.

A. The Hunger for God

"The bread of God is he which cometh down from heaven, and giveth life unto the world" (6:33). The quest for God is universal. Even the worship of pagan idols witnesses to the fact that the human soul hungers for God. That is true both in the so-called depths of heathenism, or at the heart of civilization. Man has a vast capacity for God, and therefore a vast emptiness without him. But Jesus Christ answers that hunger with these remarkable words: "The bread of God is he which cometh down from heaven, and giveth life unto the world" (6:33).

B. The Hunger for Truth

"My Father giveth you the *true* bread from heaven" (6:32). From childhood to manhood, man has an insatiable hunger for truth. The tragedy is that instead of being satisfied with the true Bread from heaven, thousands upon thousands feed upon the false bread supplied by the devil himself. Instead of feeding at the Father's table, they attempt to fill themselves with "the husks that the swine [do] . . . eat," like the prodigal son, and so ultimately "perish with hunger." Only a small minority of people come to their senses and remember the "bread enough and to spare" (Luke 15:16-17), which is to be found in Jesus Christ in the home of the Father. True Bread feeds the mind with knowledge, the heart with happiness, and the will with liberty.

Illustration

At the battle of Bothwell Brig, the ammunition of the Covenanters ran out. They were waiting for a barrel of bullets, but instead, a barrel of raisins was sent to them. So they sat down in defeat. Today, as then, the soldiers of Jesus Christ must have less confectionery and more of the truth of God.[7]

C. The Hunger for Life

He said, "I am the bread of life" (6:35). Man is hungry for life. He cannot laugh, labor, or love unless he has life. He fights for life in war, he defends life in peacetime, he works for life in daily employment, he dreams of life in sleep, he eats for life at mealtimes. His hunger is for life. And yet so many try to be satisfied with a mere existence, whereas Jesus offers the Bread of *life*!

If you are searching for life among the world's treasures and pleasures, lift your eyes to the one who holds the secret of life in all its fullness. Listen to his words: "I am the living bread which came down from heaven: if any man eat of this bread, he shall live for ever" (6:51).

Illustration

Sadhu Sundar Singh was distributing Gospels in the Central Province of India. He came to some non-Christians on the train and offered a man a copy of John's Gospel. The man took it, tore it into pieces in anger and threw the pieces out of the window. That seemed the end. But it so happened, in the providence of God, there was a man anxiously seeking for truth walking along the line that very day, and he picked up, as he walked along, a little bit of paper and looked at it, and the words on it in his own language were "The Bread of Life." He did not know what it meant; but he inquired among his friends and one of them said, "I can tell you; it is out of the Christian book. You must not read it or you will be defiled." The man thought for a moment and then said, "I want to read the book that contains that beautiful phrase!" and he bought a copy of the New Testament. He was shown where the sentence occurred—our Lord's words "I am the Bread of Life"; and as he studied the Gospel, the light flooded into his heart. He came to the knowledge of Jesus Christ, and he became a preacher of the gospel. That little bit of paper through God's Spirit was indeed the Bread of Life to him, satisfying his deepest need.[8]

Conclusion

We have seen that as the Bread of Life Christ supplies spiritual life, sustains spiritual life, and satisfies spiritual life. Now it remains for you to come to him and believe on him as the Bread of Life. Jesus said, "He that cometh to me shall never hunger; and he that believeth on me shall never thirst" (6:35). By coming, you trust in Christ; by believing, you taste of Christ. Will you trust him now, and then "taste and see that the LORD is good" (Ps. 34:8)? Trust him, then taste him, and you will go on eating and proving that Jesus Christ completely satisfies.

The Light of Life

1:1-9; 3:18-21; 8:12; 9:5

"I am the light of the world" (8:12).

Introduction

Our Lord had just attended the Jews' Feast of Tabernacles (7:2). This feast was celebrated to remind God's ancient people of their pilgrim journey through the wilderness to the Promised Land. You will remember that during their wanderings the children of Israel were supernaturally provided with manna to eat, water from the rock to drink, and the pillar of cloud and fire to shield and guide them by day and night.

In his teaching, as recorded in the Gospel of John, our Lord Jesus Christ had spoken of himself, in chapter 6, as the Bread of Life; in chapter 7, as the Water of Life; and in chapter 8, as the Light of Life.

I. The Source of Divine Light

"I am the light of the world" (8:12). This is one of the most meaningful utterances ever voiced by the Savior. This will become evident as we proceed with our study. Consider, first of all:

A. The Identity of That Source

"I am the light of the world" (8:12). In these simple yet majestic words Jesus reveals himself to be the uncreated light of deity clothed with humanity. Think again of that pillar of cloud by which the children of Israel were led in the wilderness. In appearance it was probably "like some aerial snow mountain, which is to the heavens what the iceberg is to the seas" (F. B. Meyer). At its center was the Shekinah fire of God's presence burning unceasingly. At night, the glory of this fire was diffused through the cloud to light the entire camp of Israel.

How wonderfully this illustrates the identity of our Lord Jesus Christ! Here he is shown to be truly God, and truly man. In the Shekinah glory we see his deity. In the white cumulus cloud we see his perfect humanity. During his life on earth, the vision of discerning men and women sometimes pierced that cloud and saw the glory of God. John says: "The Word was made flesh, and dwelt among us, (and we beheld his glory, the glory as of the only begotten of the Father,) full of grace and truth" (John 1:14).

Illustration

If we pick up the prism of analysis and hold it before his life, we are confronted at once with the perfections of his person. Light may be broken down into a spectrum of seven colors derived from a trinity of primary colors—red, yellow, and blue. And in this unique personality, who stands before us as the light of the world, we identify the anointed Prophet, Priest, and King.

B. *The Proximity of That Source*

Jesus declared, "As long as I am in the world, I am the light of the world" (John 9:5). If we were to discuss the source of the physical light which wakes us up in the early hours of the morning and then brightens our lives throughout the course of the day, we would conclude that it was that luminous celestial body we call the sun, which is 92,900,000 miles away. Meteorologists tell us that the sun's light reaches us at a speed of 186,300 miles per second. Our minds reel as we try to comprehend the significance of such distances and speed. But when we turn to the source of the spiritual light, our hearts are comforted by the nearness, the proximity, the immediacy, of God's light of life. "Through the tender mercy of our God; whereby the dayspring from on high hath visited us, to give light to them that sit in darkness and in the shadow of death, to guide our feet into the way of peace" (Luke 1:78-79).

Illustration

Dr. John Baillie made it a practice to open his course on the doctrine of God at Edinburgh University with these words: "Gentlemen, we must remember that in discussing God we cannot talk about Him without His hearing every word we say. We may be able to talk to our fellows, as it were, behind their backs, but God is everywhere, yes, even in this classroom."[1]

II. The Course of Divine Light

"I am the light of the world: *he that followeth me* shall not walk in darkness, but shall have the light of life" (8:12). As the light of the world, Jesus came to guide us by a straight path into the very presence of God. The Bible has much to say on this subject of light, and we need to consider the three beams that delineate the course of light:

A. The Light Beam of Knowledge

"God, who commanded the light to shine out of darkness, hath shined in our hearts, to give the light of the knowledge of the glory of God in the face of Jesus Christ" (2 Cor. 4:6). If you are prepared to receive the Lord Jesus Christ as your personal Savior, you will find that the first beam of the light of the knowledge of God in Jesus Christ would penetrate your soul. As the psalmist tells us, "For with thee is the fountain of life: in thy light shall we see light" (Ps. 36:9). John assures us, "He that doeth truth cometh to the light" (3:21).

B. The Light Beam of Fellowship

"He that followeth me shall not walk in darkness, but shall have the light of life" (8:12); and again: "If we walk in the light, as he is in the light, we have fellowship one with another, and the blood of Jesus Christ his Son cleanseth us from all sin" (1 John 1:7). There is no greater experience in all the world than walking in the light with Jesus Christ. Not only are we kept clean from every sin, but the resulting fellowship with God introduces joy, power, and blessing which continue along the whole course of our Christian life.

C. The Light Beam of Holiness

"The path of the just is as the shining light, that shineth more and more unto the perfect day" (Prov. 4:18). The light of the knowledge of Christ leads us into the light of the fellowship of Christ. The light of the fellowship of Christ, in turn, leads us into the light of holiness in Christ. The writer to the Hebrews exhorts us to "follow . . . holiness, without which no man shall see the Lord" (12:14). And in his Beatitudes, Jesus says: "Blessed are the pure in heart: for they shall see God" (Matt. 5:8). The fact is that "God is light, and in him is no darkness at all" (1 John 1:5). Consequently, if we would see God we must know the light of holiness in our lives. He says, "I am the light of the world: he that followeth me shall not walk in darkness" (8:12).

Are you prepared to follow his light beams of knowledge, fellowship, and holiness?

Illustration

Stephen Olford recounts a terrifying occasion when he was hopelessly lost just after dusk in the long grass of Central Africa. He had gone out to shoot meat for the native carriers, and, in the course of the hunt, he forgot about time and direction. Groping around in circles in the near darkness, he could make out the forms of two hunting leopards prowling around him. Visibility was too poor for him to shoot, and, in any case, there were two leopards. Only one way was open, that of prayer.

Having asked God for protection and guidance, he cupped his hands and began to call for help. His voice seemed to be strengthened by a supernatural power. Presently he had the answer to his prayers, for two headlights of their Ford truck came sweeping across the plain. Instantly, the leopards scattered, and in the straight beams of the light he was guided back to camp.

In a similar way, by means of the light beams of knowledge, fellowship, and holiness, we can be guided and helped in our walk with Jesus Christ.

III. The Force of Divine Light

"I am the light of the world: he that followeth me shall not walk in darkness, but shall have the *light of life*" (8:12). In the first chapter of this gospel the writer tells us that "in him [Christ] was life; and the life was the light of men" (1:4). In the physical realm, light is spoken of as a radiant force and a luminous energy. In the sphere of the spiritual, this divine light can be likened to:

A. A Searching Force

"Every one that doeth evil hateth the light, neither cometh to the light, lest his deeds should be reproved"

(John 3:20). As a searching force, this divine light operates like an X-ray. It exposes life and reveals character. Someone has defined light as "the agent by which objects are made visible."

How true this is of the light of God. You may be complacent and unconcerned about your life, but the moment the divine light shines into it you will become aware of your sin and cry out, like Peter, "Depart from me; for I am a sinful man, O Lord" (Luke 5:8).

Illustration

In the context of John 8, we have the story of the adulteress caught in the very act of sin. These cruel scribes and Pharisees who accused her were confident of their position when they proposed that she be stoned according to the law of Moses. Then Jesus began to expose their lives by the searching light which emanated from his own person and Word. "He that is without sin among you, let him first cast a stone at her," he demanded. And we read: "They which heard it, being convicted by their own conscience, went out one by one, beginning at the eldest, even unto the last" (John 8:7, 9). Have you allowed God's searching light to expose your heart and life?

B. A Saving Force

Listen to the testimony of the psalmist: "The LORD is my light and my salvation . . . the LORD is the strength of my life" (Ps. 27:1). For many years it has been known that certain diseases can be successfully treated by exposure to sunlight. The general physical tone of the body can be increased by the action of ultraviolet rays. It is estimated that there is a 20 percent increase in mortality wherever direct light is not enjoyed in the home, street, or office.

Similarly, there is a saving force in God's divine light. Ponder that great word in Malachi which tells us that the Lord Jesus, as "the Sun of righteousness [shall] arise with healing in his wings" (4:2). I can never recall that verse without thinking of the dark hour of Calvary, when Jesus was "made . . . sin . . . that we might be made the righteousness of God in him" (2 Cor. 5:21). Then the third day he rose again with healing and saving power in his wings. Truly, he is the light of life to all who will personally trust him.

Illustration

Bishop Taylor Smith once queried a country minister about his sermon of the previous Sunday. "Well," the humble preacher replied, "I was preaching on 'the Lord is my light,' and I pointed out to my people that light is invisible and that God is invisible, that we only know of the existence of light by the manifestation of it through the mists and in the dust of the atmosphere. It is only thus that we realize that light exists. And then I told them how we should not know God except that He shone in the person of our Lord Jesus Christ. 'He that hath seen me hath seen the Father.'" Smith said to him, "Top marks!"[2]

Only through Christ has the eternal light become a saving force to men and women who are "dead in trespasses and sins" (Eph. 2:1).

C. A Shining Force

Jesus says, "Let your light so shine before men, that they may see your good works, and glorify your Father which is in heaven" (Matt. 5:16). If he is the light of life in your experience, then that divine life must of necessity shine out through your personality and activity. Paul reminds us: "Ye were sometimes darkness, but now are ye light in the Lord: walk as children of light" (Eph. 5:8). If you have met Jesus Christ as Light of the World, then you will inevitably be a shining light for him. If your reaction to that statement is that you are only an individual, and what good is your single small light in the dark world, then let me assure you that, just as the tiniest pin prick of light is visible in a dark cave, so, whether alone or with other Christians, the shining of your light is a reminder of the greater light which "lights the world."

Conclusion

Do you know this divine light in your life? Have you personally encountered Jesus Christ? Why not receive him as the source of light, follow him as the course of light, and experience him as the force of light?

> Clear the darkened windows,
> Open wide the door;
> Let the blessed Sunshine in.

The Door of the Sheepfold
10:1-9

"I am the door: by me if any man enter in, he shall be saved, and shall go in and out, and find pasture" (10:9).

Introduction

Westerners may not understand this simile, so let us imagine that we are on holiday in the Holy Land. We visit some of those sacred and holy spots where our Lord Jesus walked, talked, and worked. Then we cross the lovely Bethlehem fields and pastures where David used to feed his sheep. Soon we come to a structure so high that we cannot scale it, and so thick that we cannot penetrate it. As we walk around it, we wonder what it can be; we see an opening, or doorway, and the hoof-marks of sheep having gone in and out, but no door. Soon a shepherd appears. A club swings from his belt, in his hand is a staff, and behind him are a hundred sheep. As he approaches we question him and to our joy find that he speaks English. When he tells us that the structure is a sheepfold, we inquire, "Do you keep your sheep here by night?" "Yes," he replies. "But how can they be safe without a door?" we ask again. With a twinkle in his eye, he stands tall and says, "*I* am the door." "Do you stay here all night?" we continue. "I do," he replies. "I build myself a shelter and sit here and keep vigil in all kinds of weather. No lion, bear, wolf, or hireling can enter my sheepfold. I am a good shepherd: I give my life for the sheep." To prove his point, he draws aside his eastern robe, and sure enough, there are scars on his arms and body. He explains that these are wounds which he has suffered as he has fought off animals while defending his sheep.

When our Lord Jesus uttered these words, he was looking beyond Calvary to resurrection life. Having suffered the wounds of battle and risen triumphantly, he stands in the doorway of God's sheepfold and says, "I am the door: by me if any man enter in, he shall be saved, and shall go in and out, and find pasture" (10:9). Here, then, we have:

I. The Door of Protection

"By me if any man enter in, he shall be saved" (or "safe," 10:9). Still with the pastoral picture in our minds, we learn from the historical background of this passage, as well as the context itself, that the shepherd offers protection from:

A. Severe Elements

"By me if any man enter in," he shall be safe (10:9). Outside there may be wind, snow, rain, or fire. Many a time, when the lightning had flashed and the prairie had caught fire, the shepherd had lost his sheep as the conflagration spread over the pasture land. Outside there was danger, death, and doom; but inside the door, safety.

"What relevance has that to today?" you ask. If I am

to declare to you the whole counsel of God I must remind you that this world is still under the abiding wrath of God. This sin-stained, stubborn, defiant world is moving on to its hour of judgment. God "hath appointed a day, in the which he will judge the world in righteousness by that man whom he hath ordained" (Acts 17:31). And "because there is wrath, beware lest he take thee away with his stroke: then a great ransom cannot deliver thee" (Job 36:18). And again: "Our God is a consuming fire" (Heb. 12:29).

Illustration

A writer describing the settlement of the American West wrote about the prairie fire. "Until the fall rains set in, the dry scorching summer months are spent in fear and suspense. Every suggestion of haze or smoke is intensely watched. But, when once fired and swept by a breeze, its speed strikes terror to man and beast as it unmercifully consumes all in its way. Many, powerless to escape, have perished, and their farms been reduced to ashes. Others, with presence of mind, seeing their danger, have stooped and fired the long dry grass at their feet, and then, as soon as the blaze had burned off a space, taken refuge by standing where the fire had been.

"Yet more solemn and terrifying will be the coming wrath and judgment of God upon this world that has crucified, and ignored the grace of, His beloved Son. It is 'reserved unto fire against the day of judgment' (2 Peter 3:7). But thanks be unto our gracious God who has provided a place of safety where the fire has already been. On Calvary's cross Christ was, as it were, enveloped in the 'fire' of God's righteous judgment to save the trembling sinner that has fled to Him for refuge (Heb. 6:18)."[1]

B. Savage Enemies

"By me if any man enter in," he shall be safe (10:9). What if the lion, the wolf, the bear, and the hireling are all outside the sheepfold? What relevance has that to this hour?

What stories we could tell today of young and old who are up against savage enemies! They intend to be pure and upright, but are constantly bruised and battered by the enemy. The Bible reminds us that "the devil, as a roaring lion, walketh about, seeking whom he may devour" (1 Peter 5:8). And Paul adds, "We wrestle not against flesh and blood, but against principalities, against powers, against the rulers of the darkness of this world, against spiritual wickedness in high places" (Eph. 6:12).

Illustration

The ant-lion is a little dark-looking creature that makes a hole in the sand, puts itself in the very center and buries itself completely out of sight, except its horn which appears like a rusty needle sticking up in the sand. An observer of its tactics wrote: "A little red ant came along seeking her food in her usual busy way. So she climbed upon the rim of the sandy cup and peeped over to investigate. Presently, suspecting danger, she turned to scramble off. Alas! it was too late; the sand rolled from under her feet, and down she went to the bottom, when in an instant that little black horn opened like a pair of shears, and 'Clip' the poor ant had lost a leg. And now the poor thing struggles to climb up, but, one leg gone, she finds it hard work. The little monster does not move or show himself. He knows what he is about. The ant has got almost to the top and liberty when the sand slips, and down she goes. 'Clip' go the shears, and another leg is gone. She struggles hard to rise, but she gets up but a little way before she slips again, and a third leg is off. She now gives up the struggle, and the lion devours her in a few minutes; and then with a flip of his tail throws the skin of the ant entirely out of the cup, and the trap is now set for another victim."

The same process is gone through with flies and other insects. No ant-lion was in sight, but the destroyer was there. The dead were pushed out of sight. "Your adversary the devil, as a roaring lion, walketh about seeking whom he may devour."[2]

C. Subtle Enticements

"By me if any man enter in," he shall be safe (10:9). Outside the sheepfold there are many enticements that would lead a sheep into danger, and even destruction, but for the watchful eye and loving care of the shepherd.

In a similar way, apart from our heavenly Shepherd, we are at the mercy of a cunning and cruel world. John says, "Love not the world, neither the things that are in the world. If any man love the world, the love of the Father is not in him. For all that is in the world, the lust of the flesh, and the lust of the eyes, and the pride of life, is not of the Father, but is of the world" (1 John 2:15-16). The apostle emphasizes here the attractions or enticements of a sinful life—"the lust of the eyes"; the appetites of a sinful life—"the lust of the flesh"; and the ambitions of a sinful life—"the pride of life."

Illustration

Stephen Olford recounts how in his college days, as part of his training in evangelism, he, with another student, was assigned London's Picadilly Circus from 11 P.M. to 6 A.M. In cabarets, vice dens, and on the streets, they found former doctors, lawyers, and other people who were caught in the allurements of modern life. They never wanted to see their families or ministers again, or be known in the circle of old friends. The subtle enticements of sin had won them over to a totally new lifestyle.

II. The Door of Purpose

"He . . . *shall go in and out,* and find pasture" (10:9). The sheep does not fulfill the purpose of the shepherd until it has entered the sheepfold. Until we have entered the door of purpose we do not fulfill the plan for which we were created. Paul reminds us that "we are his workmanship, created in Christ Jesus unto good works, which God hath before ordained that we should walk in them"

(Eph. 2:10). God has a plan for every life, and that plan is so ordered that every believer may find it, follow it, and finish it to the glory of God. The great tragedy of modern life is that many men and women are so purposeless, aimless, and thoroughly frustrated. But God promises a door of purpose to:

A. A Life of Liberty in Christ

The words "in and out" (10:9) suggest a liberated life—"the glorious liberty of the children of God" (Rom. 8:21). It is the liberty which operates only within the realm of God's purpose. It is inseparably related to the leadership of the shepherd—"He calleth his own sheep by name, and leadeth them out" (10:3).

B. A Life of Loyalty to Christ

The phrase "in and out" (10:9) further suggests an integrated life. Psychologists are agreed that one of the secrets of an integrated personality is loyalty. And who can establish loyalty like the sheep-door of our chapter? He says, "I am the good shepherd, and know my sheep"; and again: "I am the good shepherd: the good shepherd giveth his life for the sheep" (10:14, 11). It is well known that the eastern shepherd *knows* his sheep and *loves* his sheep. It has been said that such shepherds can often be blindfolded and yet distinguish the individual sheep by following the features of each animal with his fingers. In addition to this, the shepherd of the East will engage in deadly conflict in order to save them from destruction.

Illustration

The liberty in Christ and loyalty to Christ are beautifully illustrated by the following story from the early days of slavery: "A young mulatto girl was being sold at auction one day. She was a beautiful girl, tall and slender. The bidding was keen, and quickly mounted higher and higher until at last only two men were left, bidding for her ownership: the one a low, uncouth fellow who swearingly raised his bid every time to outbid the other, a quiet man of refinement. Finally the bidding stopped, and to the gentleman who had bid so very earnestly were given the papers which made him the lawful owner of the young girl. With a shove the auctioneer presented her to her new master. Proudly, defiantly, she stood before him, hating him with every part of her being. Suddenly, a change came over her face: first there was a look of pure amazement closely followed by one of utter incredulity. Her owner was ripping up the papers of ownership, and, with a smile of kindness, said to the now trembling girl, 'My dear, you are free. I bought you that I might free you.' Too stunned for speech, the girl merely stared till finally, with a cry of happiness too deep for words, she cast herself at the man's feet, and through her tears exclaimed, 'Oh, master, I'll love you and serve you for life!' What the papers of ownership could not do, the man's kindness had won completely. The Lord Jesus has loved you and has paid such a price that He might buy you for the slavery of Satan and free you. Will you not tell Him, 'Master, I'll love Thee and serve Thee for life?'"[3]

III. The Door of Provision

"He . . . shall go in and out, and find pasture" (10:9). To know Christ as the door is to enter into all the divine resources and provisions which he has prepared for them that love him. When Jesus said "pasture" or "abundant pasture" he was undoubtedly thinking of Psalm 23, for nothing could better illustrate the thought of abundant pasture than those two expressions in the opening of the psalm—"green pastures" and "still waters" (v. 2). Here is the door of provision to:

A. Spiritual Nourishment

"He maketh me to lie down in green pastures" or "pastures of tender grass" (Ps. 23:2). You will never find a hungry sheep lying down. The animal will wander even into danger and death in order to satisfy itself. But the pastures of the shepherd's provision are so plentiful that the sheep never has to wander. It finds its fill and nourishment within the provision of the shepherd. So true is this that he makes his sheep to lie down in green pastures.

Illustration

My own sheep hear my voice, He said,
A stranger they'll not heed.
In pleasant pastures they are led,
So tenderly I feed.
How can they want when near me
I lead them day by day?
How can they wander from me
When by my side they stay?

William F. Sherbert

B. Spiritual Refreshment

"He leadeth me beside the still waters" (Ps. 23:2). Those clear waters quench thirst, cleanse defilement, refresh from weariness, and calm fears. In a word, they represent the renewing work of the Holy Spirit. What a door of provision is this! All the secrets of a cleansed and settled life are to be found inside that door. No wonder the psalmist says elsewhere, "No good thing will he withhold from them that walk uprightly" (Ps. 84:11).

Now comes the question of entering this door of protection, purpose, and provision. Jesus says, "I am the door: by me if any man enter in" (10:9). What is "entering in"? It is a definite act of faith in which you take the Lord Jesus at his word and step into the fold. The Word of God reminds us that "all we like sheep have gone astray; we have turned every one to his own way" (Isa. 53:6). Why should you remain a wandering sheep outside the fold? It is important to realize that you are either in or out of the fold. On which side are you? As the chorus puts it:

> One door, and only one,
> And yet its sides are two;
> I'm on the inside,
> On which side are you?

Conclusion

Tell the Lord Jesus in simple terms that you are outside the door of protection, purpose, and provision, but that you now want to enter into that eternal sheepfold, claiming him as the Door of your life.

> Only a step to Jesus! Then why not take it now?
> Come, and thy sin confessing;
> To Him, thy Saviour, bow.
> Only a step! Only a step!
> Come, He waits for thee;
> Come, and thy sin confessing,
> Thou shalt receive a blessing:
> Do not reject the mercy
> He freely offers thee.
>
> Fanny J. Crosby

4

The Good Shepherd
10:11-18, 25-29

"I am the good shepherd: the good shepherd giveth his life for the sheep" (10:11).

Introduction

The image of the Good Shepherd has caught the imagination of men and women down through the centuries. Indeed, his role as the Good Shepherd is referred to more often than any of his other offices or ministries in the literature of Christian hymns and sermons.

In the Old Testament, Israel was a predominantly pastoral people; its religious concepts were therefore colored by the vocabulary and vocational habits familiar to a pastoral community. So we find the image of sheep and the shepherd used again and again. The figure of the shepherd is applied to Yahweh (Isa. 40:10), but it is also applied to Israel's national leaders. David is, of course, the outstanding example here (2 Sam. 5:2; Ps. 78:70, etc.).

When we come to the New Testament, however, the metaphor attains its highest prominence. This is particularly true as we come to the chapter now before us. In these verses the Lord Jesus explained what he meant by the Good Shepherd. He enlarged on:

I. The Attractiveness of His Character

"I am the good shepherd" (10:11). The literal translation is "the lovely shepherd," "the beautiful shepherd," or "the noble and genuine shepherd." How attractive is his character! Twice over this phrase "I am the good shepherd" is repeated: once in relation to his love, and the other in relation to his knowledge.

A. The Good Shepherd Loves His Sheep Infinitely

"I am the good shepherd: the good shepherd giveth his life for the sheep" (10:11). Of course, the Lord Jesus had built up a tremendous contrast before giving expression to these words. He had spoken of the marauder, or *thief,* who "[climbs] up some other way" (10:1) and is known not so much for his violence as for his subtlety and cunning. He had spoken of the *wolf,* that fearsome beast who scatters the sheep. That is how a wolf will always attack. He scatters them first, so that they are reduced to utter helplessness and loneliness. Then he destroys and devours. The Lord Jesus is neither a thief, nor a wolf; nor is he a *hireling,* a professional shepherd who only looks after the sheep for pay and takes off when he sees any danger approaching. No, our Lord is the Good Shepherd, who gives his life for the sheep; he loves his sheep infinitely.

Illustration

In St. Paul's Cathedral, London, is a life-size, marble statue of Christ in anguish on the cross. Beneath the statue are inscribed the words: "This is how God loved the world!"[1]

B. The Good Shepherd Knows His Sheep Intimately

"He calleth his own sheep by name, and leadeth them out" (10:3); and again: "I am the good shepherd, and know my sheep, and am known of mine" (10:14). There is no one who knows you so well as does the Lord Jesus. He knows you intimately and completely. There is no strength or defect in your nature that he does not know; no thought in your mind that he does not perceive; no response in your heart of which he is not aware; no longing of your being of which he is not cognizant. He knows you better than your dearest friend.

Illustration

J. H. Jowett once wrote: "In our country we do not realize the intimacy of a shepherd with his flock as they do in Syria and in parts of Southern Europe. It was my daily delight every day for many weeks and a dozen times a day, to watch a shepherd who had this almost incredibly close communion with his flock. Many times have I accompanied him through the green pastures and by the stream. If my shepherd wished to lead his sheep from one pasture to another, he went before them, and he was usually singing. I have heard his song and his low-bird-call by the watercourse, and have seen the sheep follow his course over the rocky boulders to the still waters, where they have been refreshed. At noon he would sit down in a place of shadows, and all his flock crowded around him for rest. At night, when the darkness was falling, he gathered them into the fold. We must realize an intimacy like this if we wish to understand the shepherd imagery of the Old Book."[2]

II. The Inclusiveness of His Concern

"Other sheep I have, which are not of this fold: them also I must bring, and they shall hear my voice; and there shall be one fold, and one shepherd" (10:16). Here are words to stir the heart! It was these words that motivated

David Livingstone to leave his home, and a promising career, to plunge into the dark, infested jungles of Central Africa in order to find the "sheep that were lost." Should you go into Westminster Abbey in London, England and see the stone that marks his resting place, you would find these words of Jesus inscribed upon it. The inclusiveness of the Good Shepherd's concern is seen as:

A. The Shepherd Seeks the Sheep

"Them also I must bring" (10:16). In that little word "bring" is the thought of the seeking Shepherd. He finds them because he has sought them, and desires to bring them into his fold. And there is no point of the compass that Jesus has not explored in seeking men and women who have been lost. At Calvary's cross, Jesus Christ measured every distance that the sinning and straying sheep could ever traverse.

Illustration

About 1842, George Clephane, a young Scottish lad, stepped ashore in Canada to try and begin a new life. Although only in his early twenties, George was an alcoholic. However, the change of country did not solve his problem. In company with the wrong kind of people, he spent his substance on riotous living. One cold morning he was picked up on the roadside in a state of complete collapse, the result of a drunken carousal and exposure to the elements. Shortly afterwards he died. The news of his death stirred great sorrow in his old home in Fife, but most of all in the heart of his youngest sister, Elizabeth Cecilia. She had never ceased to love the black sheep of the family, and never wavered in her conviction that God loved him too. The conviction that somehow in his dying hours, her brother had come to Jesus and been saved shaped itself into an immortal hymn:

There were ninety and nine, that safely lay,
In the shelter of the fold;
But one was out on the hills away,

Far off from the gates of gold—
Away on the mountains, wild and bare,
Away from the tender Shepherd's care.

"Lord, Thou hast here Thy ninety and nine,
Are they not enough for Thee?"
But the Shepherd made answer, "This of mine
Has wandered away from Me;
And although the road be rough and steep
I go to the desert to find My sheep."

But none of the ransomed ever knew
How deep were the waters crossed,
Nor how dark was the night that the Lord passed
    through,
Ere He found His sheep that was lost.
Out in the desert He heard its cry,
Sick and helpless, and ready to die.

"Lord, whence are those blood-drops all the way,
That mark out the mountain's track?"
"They were shed for one who had gone astray,
Ere the Shepherd could bring him back."
"Lord, whence are Thy hands so rent and torn?"
"They are pierced tonight by many a thorn."

But all through the mountains, thunder-riven,
And up from the rocky steep,
There arose a cry to the gate of heaven,
"Rejoice! I have found My sheep!"
And the angels echoed around the throne,
"Rejoice, for the Lord brings back His own!"

She died in 1869, her poem still unpublished, but it
found its way into a Glasgow paper in 1874, while Moody
and Sankey were in Scotland. Sankey bought a newspaper
at a Glasgow station and as he glanced through it hur-
riedly, his eye caught sight of Elizabeth Clephane's poem.
He cut it out for his musical scrapbook. At the noon meeting on the second day into a mission in Edinburgh the subject was "The Good Shepherd" on which Mr. Moody

preached his sermon. [Afterward] Mr. Moody asked Ira D. Sankey if he had a solo appropriate to the subject with which to close the service. Sankey, lifting up his heart in prayer to God for help, placed the little newspaper slip on the organ, and began to sing note by note the hymn to the tune to which it is still sung.[3]

B. The Shepherd Shelters the Sheep

"There shall be one . . . [flock], and one shepherd" (10:16). "Is there not already one flock down here?" someone asks. No, some are here, and some are in heaven. But when the Chief Shepherd shall appear, all the lost sheep he has ever saved will be welcomed into heaven itself and sheltered there forever. As Charles C. Ryrie puts it: "As the Good Shepherd, Christ gave His life for the sheep and became the Door into God's fold (v. 7); as the Great Shepherd (Heb. 13:20-21), He rose from the dead to care for His sheep; as Chief Shepherd (1 Peter 5:4), He will come again for His sheep."[4]

Exegesis

The misleading English translation of the word "flock" should be especially noticed. If our Lord had meant to convey the idea of the rigid enclosure into which all the scattered sheep should be gathered, he would have used the word *aulē*—"a sheepfold"—in this context. The word *poimnē* is carefully chosen. It is used here metaphorically of all Christ's followers. The King James Version is erroneous at this point and has led to serious misinterpretation of this passage. The fact is that there may be many folds, representing different nations, ages, times, and denominations, and many variations of these; but there is only one *flock* under the watchful guardianship of one shepherd. This verse has an obvious bearing on the methods of seeking Christian unity (cf. Eph. 2:11-22; Ezek. 34:23). As in John 11:52, it is Christ himself who gathers "together in one the children of God who were scattered abroad."

III. The Effectiveness of His Call

"My sheep hear my voice, and I know them, and they follow me: and I give unto them eternal life; and they shall never perish, neither shall any man pluck them out of my hand" (10:27-28). Although there is a difference of opinion among scholars as to the sequence of verses 27-30, the main thrust of the teaching is inescapable. Christ's knowledge of his sheep answers to their obedience; his new life offered to his sheep answers to their progress, and his victory gained for his sheep answers to full salvation. In essence, this is the effectual call of our heavenly Shepherd.

A. The Call Expects a Response

"My sheep hear my voice, and . . . they follow me" (10:27). Unless a person resolutely turns his back on the Good Shepherd and is determined to be independent, he will respond to the divine call; for in God's good purpose he has been elected to be sought and sheltered. There are those in every country, race, and rank who have heard and responded to that call. Each one can say:

> I heard Him call "Come, follow!"
> That was all.
> My gold grew dim,
> My soul went after Him,
> I rose and followed—
> That was all.
> Who would not follow
> If they heard Him call?
>
> Henry Wadsworth Longfellow

B. The Call Establishes a Relationship

"I give unto them eternal life; and they shall never perish, neither shall any man pluck them out of my hand" (10:28). Every sheep that comes to the Lord Jesus, confessing that he has sinned and strayed, is cleansed and immediately becomes related to him, sharing his very life.

Observe carefully that it is an *indestructible* relationship—"They shall never perish" (10:28). Without any presumption (unless it be on the truth of the Word of God), each follower of Christ should be able to say, "I am as sure of heaven as though I were already there."

Notice further that the relation is *indissoluble*—"Neither shall any man pluck them out of my hand" (10:28). There's security! Jesus said, "My Father, which gave them me, is greater than all; and no man is able to pluck them out of my Father's hand" (10:29). There's double security! Paul puts it beautifully when he says: "Your life is hid with Christ in God" (Col. 3:3). What a relationship! What a joy! What a peace! What a salvation!

Conclusion

As we have looked at this beautiful picture of our Lord and Savior Jesus Christ we have discovered that he is the Good Shepherd who died for us, the Great Shepherd who lives for us, and the Chief Shepherd who will one day come back for us. When he addresses us as "my sheep," let us respond by calling him "our Shepherd."

The Resurrection and the Life
11:20-27

"I am the resurrection, and the life: he that believeth in me, though he were dead, yet shall he live" (11:25).

Introduction

All the titles of the Lord Jesus Christ are a self disclosure of the wonder of his person and the effectiveness of his work. We come now to what is perhaps one of the most profound of his utterances—"I am the resurrection, and the life"—Christ, the quickener of our souls. The context of this utterance is tremendously important. Our Lord Jesus was speaking in the very atmosphere of death, decay and distress. Lazarus had been dead four days, and his family and friends were sorrowing. Yet with utter certainty Jesus could declare, "I am the resurrection, and the life."

I. Christ Is the Great Dispenser of Life

"I am the resurrection, and the life" (11:25). Resurrection presupposes death; death prepares for new life, and life predicates God. We come right back to the fact of God, for only God can both beget and dispense life, and the life he gives is active both in the physical and spiritual realms.

A. He Gives Physical Life

"He giveth to all life, and breath, and all things" (Acts 17:25), said the apostle Paul, when preaching on Mars' hill to the Athenians. All forms of physical life have come first from God.

It is true that scientists already have brought together certain components which have actually begun to live; even so we can only say with Johannes Kepler, the German astronomer (1571–1630), that they are "thinking God's thoughts after Him." Ultimately life comes from God alone and without God there is no life. He is the dispenser of physical life.

B. He Gives Spiritual Life

"I am come that [ye] . . . might have life, and that [ye] . . . might have it more abundantly" (or "above the common," John 10:10). This Gospel of John is the gospel of *life*. The key-word "life" appears again and again. Looking into the faces of men and women, who were on the level of mere existence, Jesus said, "The dead shall hear the voice of the Son of God: and they that hear shall live" (John 5:25). He is the dispenser of spiritual life.

Illustration

Dr. Walter Lewis Wilson in his book, *The Romance of a Doctor's Visit,* narrates that, on one occasion, going to a funeral, he had permission to ride to the cemetery with the undertaker in the hearse. As they went along, he said to the driver, a young man of thirty, "What do you suppose the Bible means by saying, 'Let the dead bury their dead'?" He replied, "There isn't a verse like that in the Bible." The Doctor assured him that there was, and he said then, "It must be a wrong translation. How could a dead person bury a dead person?" The Doctor then explained the verse by pointing out to him, "You are a dead undertaker in front of the hearse driving out to bury the dead friend at the back of the hearse. That person is dead to her family, and you are dead to God." He quoted to him John 10:10 and 1 John 5:12. The conversation resulted in the conversion of the undertaker as he accepted eternal life through faith in the Lord Jesus Christ.[1]

II. Christ Is the Great Restorer of Life

"I am the resurrection" (11:25). The word "resurrection" comes from two Greek words which mean "to cause to stand up." The thought is of someone who was standing in life, and now is lying in death. The Lord Jesus makes them stand up again.

A. Christ Restores Spiritual Life

"You hath he quickened, who were dead in trespasses and sins" (Eph. 2:1). Outside of a living union with Jesus Christ, who is the resurrection and the life, all men and women are "dead in trespasses and sins." God told Adam that in the day he violated his will and took of the forbidden fruit he would most surely die. And Adam did die—spiritually, though his physical, emotional, and rational life continued. Man was given a probationary period, but he failed, and by disobedience forfeited the very life of God. So all the sons of Adam have been born physically, emotionally, and rationally alive, but dead spiritually. "Behold, I was shapen in iniquity; and in sin did my mother conceive me" (Ps. 51:5).

You may be trained academically, you may be cultured, warm-hearted, refined, and charming, but if you are not joined in a vital union with the Lord Jesus, the resurrection, and the life, you are in a moral sepulchre—"dead in trespasses and sins" (Eph. 2:1). The wonder of the gospel message is that Christ affirms: "I am the resurrection, and the life: he that believeth in me, though he were dead, yet shall he live: and whosoever liveth and believeth in me shall never die" (11:25–26).

B. Christ Restores Physical Life

"As in Adam all die, even so in Christ shall all be made alive" (1 Cor. 15:22). In that magnificent chapter (1 Cor. 15), Paul argues his way right through to a climax. Jesus Christ has proved that he is the resurrection and the life by undergoing death and emerging in the power of his own authority. He could say of his own life, "I have power [authority] to lay it down, and I have power [authority] to take it again" (John 10:18). No one in the universe has ever voluntarily dismissed his spirit, as did Jesus at Golgotha when he cried, "It is finished" and gave up the ghost (John 19:30). From resurrection ground we hear him saying, "I am he that liveth, and was dead; and behold, I am alive for evermore" (Rev. 1:18).

And so, on the basis of the resurrection of Jesus Christ, Paul argues that every man who has ever died will live again. Those who are believers will be raised in Christ, "in a moment, in the twinkling of an eye, at the last trump." Their bodies will be changed to become like his glorious body. The "corruptible [shall] . . . put on incorruption, and [the] . . . mortal [shall] . . . put on immortality. . . . Death [will be] . . . swallowed up in victory" (1 Cor. 15:52-54).

Those who are not believers in Christ will rise just as surely, not at the first resurrection but rather at the resurrection of the unregenerate where small and great will stand before God's bar of judgment; and because of their rejection of Jesus Christ all such will be banished from his presence forever.

Illustration

When that great Christian and scientist, Sir Michael Faraday, was dying, some journalists questioned him as to his speculations for a life after death. "Speculations!" said he, "I know nothing about speculations. I'm resting on certainties. I know that my redeemer liveth, and because He lives, I shall live also."[2]

C. Christ Restores Cosmical Life

When Jesus Christ said, "I am the resurrection, and the life" (11:25), he was thinking not only of that which was spiritual and physical, but that which had cosmic proportions as well. We look around today and use the words of the old hymn, "Change and decay in all around I see." There is the rotting tree, the chill blast of winter, the minor note in the little bird's song, and creation "red in tooth and claw." Paul speaks in Romans 8 of the whole creation being subjected to wastefulness and the bondage of corruption. But one day, by virtue of the resurrection of Jesus Christ, the whole creation, which "groaneth and travaileth in pain together until now" (Rom. 8:22) will be released. Then will the birds sing, the flowers bloom and never fade again, and the whole creation will be purified and restored to a redeemed paradise: the utopia that we all yearn for.

Illustration

Some years ago a man who kept a marine aquarium saw on the surface of the water a tiny creature, appearing to be half fish, half snake, not an inch long, writhing as if in distress. With convulsive efforts it bent its head to tail, now on this side, now on that, springing in circles with a strength amazing in a creature so small. The observer bent over to remove it lest it should sink and die and pollute the clear waters, when, in a moment, its skin split from end to end, and there sprang out a delicate fly with slender legs and pale lavender wings. Balancing itself for a moment on its discarded skin, it preened its gossamer wings and then flew out of an open window. This phenomenon made a deep and lasting impression on the one who watched. He learned once again that *nature hints at the truth of the resurrection.*

III. Christ Is the Great Preserver of Life

"I am the resurrection, and the *life*" (11:25). Having restored life he preserves it. That is an added benefit of redemption. Adam in innocence was on trial, and having failed, he forfeited life. But now life has been restored, and our Lord Jesus Christ has made it possible for it never to be lost again. Through grace he has become our very life, and to lose life is to lose him, and that cannot be, for every believer shares the life of Christ. As every branch is part of the vine, so we are members one of another.

A. Christ Preserves Us by His Protective Word

"Man shall not live by bread alone, but by every word that proceedeth out of the mouth of God" (Matt. 4:4); and again, the words of the Lord Jesus: "The words that I speak unto you, they are spirit, and they are life" (John 6:63). It is difficult to understand how anyone who calls himself a Christian does not have an insatiable appetite for the Word of God. "As newborn babes, desire the sincere milk of the word, that ye may grow thereby," says Peter in his first epistle (2:2). A little baby will cry for milk, and there is something wrong if a spiritual child does not seek his Father's provision day by day.

Creation, too, is held together by the outgoing of that same word. "Through faith we understand that the worlds were framed by the word of God" (Heb. 11:3), and He upholds "all things by the word of his power"

(Heb. 1:3). When men and women are raised to life from the grave, it will be by the power of that same word.

B. Christ Preserves Us by His Redemptive Work

Jesus said, "Except ye eat the flesh of the Son of man, and drink his blood, ye have no life in you" (John 6:53); and again: "He that eateth my flesh, and drinketh my blood, dwelleth in me, and I in him" (John 6:56). This is the redemptive work of Christ by which life is maintained. It was at the cross that life was first made available, and it is there that life is maintained.

Illustration

Herbert Lockyer in the *London Christian Herald* tells of a friend of his in Glasgow who "found himself in Barlinnie prison because of his sin. He was given to drunkenness, became a sot, and grieved the heart of his godly mother. After serving his term of imprisonment, he found his way back again to the old home, and the mother who loved him pleaded with him to sign his pledge. But, like the honest man he was, he said, 'No, Mother, I have signed enough pledges to paper the wall; I need something more than a pledge. I need a power that can make me a sober man, and change my life.' Growing desperate, his mother took a knife and opened one of her veins, and dipping a pen into her flowing blood, she said, 'Sinclair, sign it with your mother's blood, and that may help you.' I heard him say one night before a crowded audience. 'What the blood of my mother could not do, the blood of Jesus Christ accomplished,' and that man tonight is preaching the Gospel of the Redeemer."[3]

C. Christ Preserves Us by His Directive Will

"Because I live, ye shall live also" (John 14:19). What comfort these words must have brought to the disciples. There they were, on the eve of the crucifixion. Jesus had told them he was going to die. But they had to be reminded that he was also the resurrection, and

the life; and that it was his will that they, too, should
live. The Lord Jesus will see to it that while he lives we
shall never die. He says, "Whosoever liveth and believeth in me shall never die" (11:26).

Conclusion

How may we know this life? The answer is twofold:
first, there must be *an acceptance of Christ*—"He that
believeth in me" (11:25). There must be union with a person, not a doctrine. "This is the record, that God hath
given to us eternal life, and this life is in his Son" (1 John
5:11). Second, there must be *an abiding in Christ*—he that
"liveth and believeth in me shall never die" (11:26).
Abiding in him through his Word, through his cross, and
through his will means life, and life "more abundant."
Paul's testimony was, "I live; yet not I, but Christ liveth
in me: and the life which I now live in the flesh I live by
the faith of the Son of God, who loved me, and gave himself for me" (Gal. 2:20).

The Way, the Truth, the Life
13:36–14:6

"I am the way, the truth, and the life" (14:6).

Introduction

When Thomas looked into the face of Jesus Christ and pleaded, "Lord, . . . how can we know the way?" (14:5), he voiced the deepest need of the human soul. His homesickness for heaven was, in the final analysis, a longing for Christ. The hymnwriter was correct when he wrote, "Where Jesus is, 'tis heaven there." The fact is that Christ had become the answer to every need in the experience of Thomas, and he dreaded the possibility of separation from his source of help. So he cried, "Lord, . . . how can we know the way?" (14:5). In other words, "How can we know you as an ever-present reality?" The Savior's reply was a final answer, not only for Thomas, but for all men in every age. Jesus said:

I. I Am the Way In Order That Men Might Be Saved

By nature man has lost himself in the maze of sin. "All we like sheep have gone astray; we have turned every one to his own way" (Isa. 53:6). The express purpose for which the Son of man came into the world was "to seek and to save that which was lost" (Luke 19:10). Christ, therefore, has become the "way" that men might be saved.

A. Christ Is the Only Way to Be Saved

"I am the way," said Christ, "no man cometh unto the Father, but by me" (14:6). While there are as many ways to Christ as there are feet to tread them, there is only *one* way to God; that is, Christ himself. This is not a popular doctrine, and, therefore, not generally accepted, but it remains a fact.

If liberalism had its say, it would tell us that there are many ways to the Father; for instance, the way of nature, the way of aesthetics, the way of charity. If materialism had its say, it would tell us that the way to the Father is through the improvement of man's environment, until he attains to perfection. If ecclesiasticism had its say, it would tell us that the way to the Father is through the sacraments, the rites, and good works. But all these, who undertake to climb over into the fold by "some other way," are thieves and robbers. There is only one way to the Father: it is Christ. He is the *only* way to be saved. There is only one way to get into heaven, and that is by Jesus Christ, *the only way.*

Illustration

A man, wont to trust in his own merit for salvation, dreamed one night that he was constructing a ladder which was to reach from earth to heaven. Whenever the dreamer did a good deed the ladder went up higher. So in the course of years the ladder passed out of sight of the earth, clear up into the clouds. But at last when the competent builder was about to step off the topmost round onto the floor of heaven, a voice cried, "He that climbeth up some other way is a thief and a robber!" Down came the ladder with a crash. The startled dreamer awoke. He had learned his lesson. He saw that he must get salvation from Jesus Christ, for his own self-righteousness, inadequate to fulfill the whole law of God, availed not.[1]

B. Christ Is the Open Way to Be Saved

"I am the way" (14:6), says Christ. A way is that which makes movement in some specific direction possible. Without the work of Christ at Calvary there would be no way to heaven. He is not only the pathfinder, but the path along which he invites us to walk. He has done all that is necessary in order that we might arrive safely.

Illustration

Stephen Olford recounts how his missionary father was preaching in the villages of Angola, Africa. After one memorable meeting with a chief and his men, Frederick Olford asked if there were other villages that would give him the same kind of welcome and hearing. The chief said "Yes, a village right through this forest." "But," replied his father, "I don't know the way." "That is no problem," assured the chief. With that he called one of his men and instructed him to take the missionary through the forest to the adjacent village. After traveling for several hours, Olford said, "We have been traveling a long time and we haven't arrived. Do you really know the way?" The man grinned, took his ax from his shoulder, and said, "White man, do you see the marks on those trees there? I made those marks when I blazed the trail. Do you see this ax I hold in my hand? With this ax I cut the way through this forest. Do you see these marks on my body? They are wounds I suffered when I first pushed my way through the undergrowth to make the way." And then standing his full height and tapping his massive chest, the African said with ringing confidence, "I am the way; follow me."

The Lord Jesus points to the marks of his passion and

says, "These are the wounds I suffered when I made the way to heaven through the dark jungle of sin. I am the way; follow me."

II. I Am the Truth In Order That Men Might Be Sure

When Jesus declared "I am the truth" he gave expression to one of the most profound concepts we find in Scripture. In those words he claimed to be the expression of the absolute truth about God's nature, God's idea of humanity, the relation between moral beings and God. In essence, the Lord Jesus claimed to be:

A. Truth Embodied in the Incarnate Word

"I am the . . . truth" (14:6). In the last analysis, truth is a moral abstraction and can only exist in relation to a person—a person who can somehow stand as its representation and end. That person is Christ. Aristotle once said, "Mind, as it came from its Maker, is organized for truth, as the eye to perceive the light, and the ear to hear sounds." That is why the man who finds Christ knows that he has found truth. There is a reality within him which witnesses to truth.

Illustration

Stephen Olford recounts an occasion during World War II when he met a young naval officer by the name of John whose conversion story was quite dramatic. While a vociferous atheist, he had been involved in action with his fellow sailors. The bombing raid had taken a serious toll of life, including his roommate, who was a Christian. Before that fatal day he had often debated, and even derided, his Christian friend, but failed to shake his faith or rob him of his composure and cheerfulness. As John returned to his bunk that day he saw his roommate's Bible lying open. With sorrow in his heart, and a deep longing to know the secret of the faith his Christian friend possessed, he picked up the Bible and began to read the Gospel of John.

As he turned the pages, the Spirit of God worked in his heart, and before he was through the twenty-one chapters he was born again.

Olford asked him if he still had intellectual problems. "Oh, yes, I do," replied John, "and one by one they are being resolved as I continue to read God's Word. But I have no doubt that Jesus Christ is the truth. In meeting and knowing Him, I have experienced a transforming reality I never knew before."

Amplification

Christ is the truth because he is the self-revelation of God which has been manifested (John 14:7, 9), the light that has come into the world without the appropriation of which salvation is not obtained (compare John 1:14, 8:32, 14:17; 1 John 5:6 in connection with John 14:26; Eph. 4:21). "As being the perfect revelation of God the Father: combining in himself and manifesting all divine *reality*— whether in the *being,* the *law,* or the *character* of God—he embodies what men ought to *know* and *believe* of God; what they should *do* as children of God, and what they should *be.*"[2]

B. Truth Embodied in the Inspired Word

"I am the . . . truth" (14:6). When Jesus uttered these words he was not only thinking of the testimony of the Old Testament, but predicting the witness of the New Testament, for he could say, "Search the scriptures; for in them ye think ye have eternal life: and they are they which testify of me" (John 5:39). And then he added: "The Holy Ghost, whom the Father will send in my name, he shall teach you all things, and bring all things to your remembrance, whatsoever I have said unto you" (John 14:26). In essence the Bible is the crib that contains the Christ.

Illustration

Walter F. Burke, former general manager of Project Mercury and Gemini and vice-president of the McDonnell

Douglas Corporation, teaches Sunday school in his church. In an interview he declared: "I have found nothing in science or space exploration to compel me to throw away my Bible or to reject my Savior, Jesus Christ, in whom I trust. The space age has been a factor in the deepening of my own spiritual life. I read the Bible more now. I get from the Bible what I cannot get from science— the really important things of life."[3] A testimony like this encourages us to rest upon the written Word of God with quiet assurance.

III. I Am the Life In Order That Men Might Be Strong

By this term "life" the Lord Jesus intended to convey something far more than temporal life. He was offering:

A. Abundant Life

Jesus could say, "I am come that they might have life, and that they might have it more abundantly" (John 10:10). How different is this conception of life to the one commonly attached to Christianity! Here indeed is life in its fullness, life with a capital L.

Some scientists have hazarded the speculation that the origin of life on this planet came with the falling upon it of a fragment of a meteor with a speck of organic life upon it from which all else has developed. Whether that is true or not in regard to the physical life, it is absolutely true in the case of spiritual life. This abundant life of which we are speaking has come from heaven itself, by way of the incarnation, into the clouds and depressions of our terrestrial atmosphere. It is the eternal germ which Jesus has planted in the heart of his redeemed people to spread forever. It is a quality of life which can cope with any situation, under any set of circumstances.

Illustration

Henry M. Stanley, the man who found David Livingstone in Africa and lived with him for some time, gives this testimony: "I went to Africa as prejudiced as the biggest atheist in London. But there came for me a long time for reflection. I saw this solitary old man there and asked myself, 'How on earth does he stop here—is he cracked, or what? What is it that inspires him?' For months after we met I found myself wondering at the old man carrying out all that was said in the Bible—'Leave all things and follow Me.' But little by little his sympathy for others became contagious; my sympathy was aroused; seeing his piety, his gentleness, his zeal, his earnestness, and how he went about his business, I was converted by him, although he had not tried to do it."[4] This is an example of what Jesus meant when he said, "I am come that [ye] . . . might have life, and that [ye] . . . might have it [above the common]." This is life indeed!

B. Triumphant Life

"In him was life; and the life was the light of men. And the light shineth in darkness; and the darkness comprehended it not" (John 1:4-5). Sin and holiness can never stay together for long. If you would be truly happy you must be truly holy, and the secret is bound up with this triumphant life. Paul knew this kind of life, for he could say, "The law of the Spirit of life in Christ Jesus hath made me free from the law of sin and death" (Rom. 8:2). This spiritual life not only purifies personal life, but, like salt, has the potent quality of arresting corruption in the various aspects of social and national life.

Illustration

Lloyd George once said: "I have always found throughout my career that, when there was a big moral question to settle in England, when the chapel bells began to ring in unison, the fight was over."

Conclusion

Jesus said, "I am the way, the truth, and the life." Without the way there is no going; without the truth there is no knowing; without the life there is no living. "I am the way which you should pursue; the truth which you should believe; the life which you should hope for." (Thomas à Kempis, *The Imitation of Christ*).

7

The True Vine

15:1-8, 16

"I am the true vine, and my Father is the husbandman" (15:1).

Introduction

Authorities are disagreed as to what may have prompted our Lord's use of the metaphor of the vine. Some say it was the celebration of the communion feast. Others suggest that when Jesus left the supper table and went down to the brook Kidron he had to pass the temple, and on the gate of that glorious building was sculptured the golden vine. He might have stopped there and given this wonderful discourse. But it is more likely that as our Lord walked down the slopes of the hill of Zion to the Garden of Gethsemane, he would have noticed the surrounding vineyards. Just about that time those vines would have been pruned, and the dead wood would be burning all over the valley. Looking out upon those vines, and the dead or barren branches that were being burned, Jesus uttered these words, "I am the true vine, and my Father is the husbandman. Every branch in me that beareth not fruit he taketh away: and every branch that beareth fruit, he purgeth it, that it may bring forth more fruit" (15:1-2). The Lord Jesus invites us to consider:

I. The Identity of the Vine

"I am the true vine" (15:1). As he spoke these words his listeners would recall the utter failure of God's ancient people, the Jews. They had never reached the fulfillment of God's purpose; but here was one who was calling himself "the true vine."

As we examine the word "true," we discover that it occurs something like twenty-nine times in the New Testament, twenty-one of these being in the Gospel of John. It means "perfect," "ideal," "noble," and is the root of the adverb "verily." The old Puritans often used the word "very"; when a man was true, trusted, and worthy of favor he was called "the very man." This is the source of the phrase in the Nicene Creed: "very God of very God; very man of very man." Here, then, is the true vine. Notice:

A. His Perfect Formation

"I am the true vine" (15:1). What is the first thing a vinedresser looks for? He looks at a vine's branches. Are they characterized by pliancy? Do they move and grow thickly and symmetrically over the trellises and supports? Perhaps there is no really perfect plant on earth, in the last analysis, but Jesus says here: "You will identify the perfect vine by its formation. I am that vine."

As we confront our Lord Jesus Christ, we find that his character is the most balanced of anyone who ever lived, or will live upon this earth. When John looked upon him, with his colleagues, he was compelled to declare, "The Word [became] . . . flesh, and dwelt among us, (and we beheld his glory, the glory as of the only begotten of the Father,) full of grace and truth" (John 1:14).

Amplification

Amplify by exalting the person of our wonderful Lord. The test of every true character is, first of all, purity and, second, influence upon mankind. Judged by both these tests Jesus Christ is unique, incomparable, and utterly other. Concerning his purity, he could look into the faces of friends and foes and say, "Which of you convinceth me of sin?" (John 8:46). And they dare not raise a voice. The evil spirit said, "I know . . . who thou art, the Holy One of God" (Mark 1:24). Judas said, "I have . . . betrayed the innocent blood" (Matt. 27:4). "In him is no sin," say the apostles; He "did no sin"; He "knew no sin" (1 John 3:5; 1 Peter 2:22; 2 Cor. 5:21). And as for his influence upon mankind, no one has influenced literature, art, music, culture, education, science, and the human personality like Jesus Christ the Son of God.

B. His Perfect Foliage

"I am the true vine" (15:1). As the vinedresser examines the foliage of the grapevine, with its almost translucent leaves, he looks for health and loveliness, green and thrifty growth. Artists will tell you that, because of their sheer beauty, magic, and intrinsic worth as aesthetic objects, vine leaves and the bloom on a grape cluster are among the most challenging and appealing subjects of art throughout history.

As we look at Jesus Christ through the words of this wonderful Book, we find that of all the persons who have ever lived he is the only perfect one. Of course, if we are blind in sin, conceited and proud, and have never been united to the living vine, we may be like the Jewish people of his day who saw "no beauty that

[they] . . . should desire him" (Isa. 53:2). But having eyes anointed by the Holy Spirit, we have to declare, in the words of the Song of Solomon, "He is altogether lovely . . . the chiefest among ten thousand" (Song of Sol. 5:16, 10). In him there is beauty, grace and fragrance. Throughout the world the vine is recognized as a symbol of fruitfulness, nourishment, and beauty. God has chosen this as the symbol of the loveliness of the Lord Jesus.

Illustration

The following is a translation of a letter sent by Publius Lentulus to the Roman senate during the Roman Empire period. "There appeared in these days a man of great virtue, named Jesus Christ, who is yet among us; of the Gentiles accepted for a prophet of truth; but his disciples call him the Son of God. He raiseth the dead, and cureth all manner of disease. A man of stature somewhat tall and comely, with a very reverend countenance, such as the beholder must both love and fear.

"In reproving, he is terrible; in admonishing, courteous and fair-spoken; pleasant in conversation, mixed with gravity. It cannot be remembered that any have seen him laugh, but many have seen him weep; in speaking, very temperate, modest, and wise; a man of singular beauty, surpassing the children of men."[1]

C. His Perfect Fruitfulness

"I am the true vine" (15:1). The grapes of Eshcol were so enormous that they could weigh anywhere from twelve to fifteen pounds a cluster. When Joshua, Caleb, and the other ten explorers went into the valley of Eshcol and cut those clusters of grapes, two men had to carry their immense weight on a pole. As you know, crushed grapes make a wonderful drink and dried grapes make a wonderful feast. In our Lord Jesus Christ there is complete sustenance for everyone who will come to him. He is the true vine, perfect in formation, in foliage, and fruitage.

Amplification

Amplify by underscoring the perfections of Christ. Jesus said, "I am the . . . vine [the perfect]; and my Father is the husbandman" (15:1). Consider the words of God the Father, who is infallible in his judgment, searching in his wisdom, and inscrutable in his discernment. On two occasions he broke into time to speak concerning his Son. Looking back over his private life, at the age of thirty, when he was baptized in Jordan, God could say of him, "This is my beloved Son, in whom I am well pleased" (Matt. 3:17). Three years later, after his public ministry had been scrutinized by foe, fiend, and friend, on the Mount of Transfiguration, God could declare yet once again, "This is my beloved Son, in whom I am well pleased; hear ye him" (Matt. 17:5).

II. The Dependency of the Vine

"I am the vine, ye are the branches" (15:5). Although he is the perfect vine, he is dependent upon us as the branches for the human expression of his life. He longs to see reproduced in us as individuals, and the church as a corporate body, all that he was in his incarnate perfection. Because of sin this perfection will not be consummated until we see him in glory. In the meantime, however, he continues his sanctifying work in us day by day. How we reveal his life depends on what kind of branches we are.

A. The Fruitful Branch

"Every branch that beareth fruit, he purgeth it, that it may bring forth more fruit" (15:2). The function of the branch is to bear fruit, and so it needs to be pruned to become more and more fruitful.

How often men and women have come to me and said, "I am interested in being a Christian, but there is one problem that haunts me. Why is it that Christian people seem to suffer so much? If they are God's own people, why does he not protect them from suffering?"

God has his heavenly logic and purpose in our suffering. Says George MacDonald: "Jesus Christ, the Son of God, suffered, not that we might be saved from suffering, but that our suffering might be like His." If the world is going to know a redemption, it must be through the work of the cross, and that means death—an unpopular but necessary doctrine for Christian people. There must be a Calvary before there can be a Pentecost. There must be a cutting back of the self-life, so that the Christ-life may burst forth.

Illustration

Dr. John Wilson, writing in *The Christian,* said that he once "heard Booth-Tucker say that he preached in Chicago one day, and out from the throng a burdened toiler came and said to him, before all the audience: 'Booth-Tucker, you can talk like that about how Christ is dear to you and helps you; but if your wife was dead, as my wife is, and you had some babies crying for their mother, who would never come back, you would not say what you are saying.'

"Just a few days later, he lost his beautiful and nobly gifted wife in a railway wreck, and the body was brought to Chicago and carried to the Salvation Army barracks for the funeral service. Booth-Tucker at last stood up after the funeral service and said: 'The other day when I was here, a man said I could not say Christ was sufficient if my wife were dead and my children were crying for their mother. If that man is here, I tell him that Christ is sufficient. My heart is all crushed. My heart is all bleeding. My heart is all broken, but there is a song in my heart, and Christ put it there.'

"That man was there, and down the aisle he came, and fell down beside the casket, and said, 'Verily, if Christ can help us like that, I will surrender to Him.' He was saved there and then."[2]

B. The Barren Branch

"Every branch in me that beareth not fruit he taketh away" (15:2). If the fruitful branch represents the spiritual man, the barren branch speaks of the carnal man. There are too many carnal Christians who are not prepared for the knife, for the suffering which brings the glory. But notice the solemn words, "He taketh away" (15:2). This is not a reference to eternal damnation, for these words are spoken of the Christian, but rather a warning concerning a possible cutting off of the physical life.

Exegesis

Explain "taketh away." "The word may mean this literally (as "remove" in [John] 11:39) and would therefore be a reference to the physical death of fruitless Christians [Acts 5:6, 10]; 1 Cor. 11:30, [and 1 John 5:16]; or it may mean lift up (as "picked up" in [John] 8:59) which would indicate that the vinedresser encourages and makes it easier for the fruitless believer, hoping he will respond and begin to bear fruit."[3]

C. The Withered Branch

"If a man abide not in me, he is cast forth as a branch, and is withered; and men gather them, and cast them into the fire, and they are burned" (15:6). Notice that when Jesus speaks here of the withered branch, he does not say "Every branch *in me*." It is a branch, evidently, which has a defect; a branch that is not properly secure in the vine. There is a blockage, or a breakage, and the life of the vine is not flowing through it.

What happens to the withered branches? They are burned. The symbolism here is terrifying, if you take it seriously, and there is no other way to take it. Who gathers the branches, how they are burned, and what it means, is left in silence, without any explanation. All we know is that Scripture expounds Scripture, and if we are to understand this picture at all we have to remember that there is a place for withered branches:

it is separation forever from the presence of God. It is spoken of as "the lake of fire" (Rev. 20:14) that burns with inextinguishable flame. If the horrifying symbolism of that does not cause us to fear in the presence of God, may he have mercy on our souls!

Amplification

How then may we be united to the vine and become fruitful branches? Jesus replies, "Abide in me, and I in you" (15:4). This simply means *the acceptance of Christ*—"I in you" (15:4). You must open the door of your heart, and receive the Lord Jesus into your life now. "He that is joined unto the Lord is one spirit" (1 Cor. 6:17). With the acceptance of Christ there must be *the reliance on Christ*—"Abide in me" (15:4). Before there can be communion there must be union. Union is the acceptance of Christ, and communion continues by reliance on Christ. In order to abide in Christ you must feed upon his Word and get to know him; then bask in the sunshine of his love, drawing from him the resources, the very life, of the vine.

III. The Fertility of the Vine

"Herein is my Father glorified, that ye bear much fruit; so shall ye be my disciples" (15:8); and again: "Ye have not chosen me, but I have chosen you, and ordained you, that ye should go and bring forth fruit, and that your fruit should remain" (15:16). The whole purpose of the fertility of the Vine is that God should be glorified. Indeed, that is the whole purpose of our lives. We are to "glorify God, and to enjoy him for ever." There are two ways in which God is glorified, in relation to the fertility of the vine. The first is:

A. Christian Discipleship

"Herein is my Father glorified, that ye bear much fruit; so shall ye be my disciples" (15:8). A disciple is a person who receives not only the authority, but the sovereignty, of his Lord; one who disciplines his life in obedience, to bear fruit to the glory of God. Jesus Christ wants men and women who will follow him closely, loyally, cost what it will, even if it means the pruning knife.

Illustration

Henry Drummond, preacher and author, once introduced an address to a select West End club in London with these words: "Ladies and gentlemen, the entrance fee into the kingdom of heaven is nothing: the annual subscription is everything."[4]

B. Christian Apostleship

"Ye have not chosen me, but I have chosen you, and ordained you, that ye should go and bring forth fruit, and that your fruit should remain" (15:16). Christian apostleship is one of the great needs in the Christian church today. The biblical use of this word "apostle" is confined to the New Testament where it occurs seventy-nine times. It literally means "to send." Christ was an apostle, a "sent one"; the twelve were apostles. Paul and others were apostles, and it is clear from the Word of God that we can be apostles today.

Alongside the distinctive and more technical use of the word is the employment of it in the sense of the messenger (Phil. 2:25; 2 Cor. 8:23). Right through to the end of time God needs messengers who will go out to bring forth fruit that will remain.

Illustration

While David Brainerd, one of the most celebrated of our missionaries, was laboring among the poor, benighted Indians on the banks of the Delaware, he once said, "I care not where I live, or what hardships I go through, so that I can but gain souls to Christ. While I am asleep, I dream of these things; as soon as I awake, the first thing I think of is this great work. All my desire is the conversion of sinners, and all my hope is in God."[5]

Conclusion

We conclude as we started, with the thought of Christ the perfect vine. Just as he could reveal the Father perfectly in his incarnation, so we are called upon to reveal our Savior through our mortal bodies. The only way in which this can be accomplished is by abiding in him, so that his life and fruit may be seen in us. God save us from being barren, or withered, branches! God make us fruitful branches, bearing not only "fruit," "more fruit," but "much fruit" (15:2, 8).

Part 2

God Alive in Miracles
from the Gospel of John

The Changing of Water into Wine:
The Glory of Christ
2:1-11

Introduction

The miracles of the New Testament are recorded to illustrate the glory of our Lord Jesus Christ. Particularly is this so in the Gospel of John, where we read of seven miracles before the resurrection and one after the resurrection. These miracles John calls "signs," because they each have special significance and a message to teach.

Out of all the miracles our Lord performed it is significant that the first one had to do with a wedding. This is because marriage, at its best, is the highest point of human realization. God's great design is consummated when a man and woman are made one in fellowship, joy, and blessing. At this point of highest achievement and realization, however, there was a threatened failure. Indeed, that is often the case, for as the psalmist says, "Verily every man at his best state is altogether vanity" (Ps. 39:5). It was at this point that the Lord Jesus broke into the scene and turned what would have been gloom into glory.

I. The Presence of Christ in Human Life

"Both Jesus was called, and his disciples, to the marriage" (2:2). When Jesus first appeared in his ministry, it was not at a synagogue or church, nor at a funeral, but at a wedding. There, in the midst of human joys, he showed that the gospel speaks to the happiest and gladdest experiences of life, for the gospel of our Lord Jesus Christ is "Good News." It is the Good News spelled out to needy men and women.

Notice, in the context of the previous chapter, that the presence of the Lord Jesus manifesting his glory was the presence of "grace and truth." "The Word was made flesh, and dwelt among us, (and we beheld his glory, the glory as of the only begotten of the Father) full of grace and truth" (John 1:14).

A. His Presence Always Elevates

"The only begotten of the Father, full of grace" (John 1:14). "Grace" brings liberation and salvation. "The grace of God that bringeth salvation hath appeared to all men" (Titus 2:11); and again: "Sin shall not have dominion over you: for ye are not under the law, but under grace" (Rom. 6:14). Grace always saves and elevates. The presence of the Lord Jesus lifted that scene of threatened sorrow and tragedy into a wedding that has become known through history as an example of joy and celebration because of his miracle-working presence.

Illustration

Africaner, the notorious Hottentot chief, was the terror of the whole country. He carried on a cruel and constant warfare with his neighbors, stealing cattle, burning kraals, capturing women and children and killing his enemies. When Robert Moffatt, as a messenger from the Prince of Life, started for Africaner's kraal, friends warned him that the savage monster would make a drum-head of his skin and a drinking cup of his skull, that no power could change such a savage. But Moffatt went to the chief and spoke to him the word of life. It entered the heathen heart and Africaner lived. He left the environment of death, was loosened from the bands of the grave, and became a Christian chief. When a Dutch farmer, whose uncle Africaner had killed, saw the converted Hottentot he exclaimed: "Oh God, what cannot thy grace do! What a miracle of thy power!"[1]

B. His Presence Always Educates

"The only begotten of the Father, full of . . . truth" (John 1:14). If grace saves, then truth sanctifies; and the presence of the Lord Jesus at that wedding was a sanctifying influence. He brought the happy experience of that young couple right up to the standard of his immediate presence. Nothing happened at that feast without his approval and control.

In his high priestly petition, the Lord Jesus prayed, "Sanctify them through thy truth: thy word is truth" (John 17:17). If your life is to be lived at the highest level; if you want the sweetness and sanctifying power of God to operate, then you must invite the Lord Jesus into your life. His grace will save, his truth will sanctify.

Illustration

If we work upon marble, it will perish; if on brass, time will efface it; if we rear temples, they will crumple into dust; but if we work upon immortal minds, and imbue them with principles, with the just fear of God and love of

our fellow men, we engrave on those tablets something
that will brighten to all eternity.[2]

II. The Power of Christ in Human Life

"This beginning of miracles did Jesus in Cana of
Galilee" (2:11). "The miracles of Jesus are called signs
by John in order to emphasize the significance of the
miracles rather than the miracles themselves. They revealed [the] various aspects of the person or work of Christ
(here His glory), and their purpose was to encourage faith
in His followers."[3] The glory of Christ's power was demonstrated in a threefold manner:

A. He Restored Order

"They have no wine" (2:3). It seems that Mary was
there before Jesus (the tense used in the Greek suggests
that she was already there); and it is possible that she
was in charge of the wedding festivities. Therefore, a
failure would be a reflection on her, and for a moment
she panicked. "They have no wine. The wine has
failed!" she said to Jesus—and she expected a miracle
of him. He was her son, it was true, but she had already
pondered much in her heart what kind of man he was.
She knew that he was none other than the Son of God,
the Messiah, so she broke in upon him and said,
"Won't you do something about it?" "Woman," he said,
"leave it to me. My hour is not yet come. Be confident
that I have a plan for all of this, and at the right
moment I will act."

Exegesis

John 2:4. The word "woman" *(gunē)* is used of a female,
unmarried or married. As employed in our text it car-
ries no tone of reproof or severity, but of endearment
and respect. The Lord Jesus used the same form of
address when he spoke from Calvary's cross and said,

"Woman, behold thy son!" and to the disciple, "Behold thy mother!" (John 19:26-27).

There was panic and chaos at the wedding, but the Lord Jesus brought order out of it. And when he comes into a life he brings order out of chaos. God had a plan for his Son, and he walked every moment and hour according to that divine program. He has a plan for your life, too. Have you that divine sense of direction and destiny in your life?

Illustration

The minister who was drilling Sunday school students in catechism asked, "What is a miracle?" A little girl put up her hand and replied, "Something we can't do, but Jesus can."

So often when faced with a chaotic situation we throw up our hands and say, "I quit." This is when we ought to remember that Jesus specializes in bringing order out of chaos. We can't, but he can!

B. He Released Nature

"Draw out now, and bear unto the governor of the feast" (2:8), and even as they drew the water it turned to wine. Having been told to "fill the waterpots with water" (2:7), the servants filled them to the brim in complete obedience. Then the miracle happened. As the water was poured out it could be seen that it had turned to wine!

What Jesus did here was to speed up the processes of nature. What is wine but the dew and rain of heaven sucked up through the roots and branches into the cluster of grapes until it reddens to the wine we all recognize? It took Jesus only an instant, not a season, to produce that wine. He released nature from its bondage of time.

Why is the universe slowed down and delayed in its unfolding of natural beauties and wonders? Because of the bondage of corruption (Rom. 8:21). When Adam sinned in the Garden he brought the curse of sin upon creation, and ever since, creation has groaned under the bondage of corruption, awaiting that glad day when, released from bondage, nature will perform as God intended it to do.

Illustration

William Jennings Bryan was once eating a piece of watermelon and was struck by its beauty. He relates: "I took some of the seeds and weighed them and found that it would require some 5,000 seeds to weigh a pound. And then I applied mathematics to a forty-pound melon. One of these seeds, put into the ground, when warmed by the sun and moistened by the rain goes to work; it gathers from somewhere 200,000 times its own weight and forcing this raw material through a tiny stem, constructs a watermelon. It covers the outside with a coating of green; inside of the green it puts a layer of white, and within the white a core of red, and all through the red it scatters seeds, each one capable of continuing the work of reproduction.

"Everything that grows tells a like story of infinite power. Why should I deny that a divine hand fed a multitude with a few loaves and fishes when I see hundreds of millions fed every year by a hand which converts the seeds scattered over the field into an abundant harvest? We know that food can be multiplied in a few months' time. Shall we deny the power of the Creator to eliminate the element of time, when we have gone so far in eliminating the element of space?"[4]

C. He Reversed Failure

"When the ruler of the feast had tasted the water that was made wine, and knew not whence it was: (but the servants which drew the water knew;) the governor of the feast called the bridegroom, and saith unto him, Every man at the beginning doth set forth good wine; and when men have well drunk, then that which is worse: but thou hast kept the good wine until now" (2:9-10). The Lord Jesus turned failure into success, crisis into creativity, tragedy into triumph, poverty into plenty, water into wine.

When man provides anything, he always supplies the best at first, and then an inferior quality. But when Jesus Christ comes into a life he starts with the best, and then continues to do "above all that we ask or think" (Eph. 3:20). He alone can turn failure into victory.

III. The Purpose of Christ in Human Life

"This beginning of miracles did Jesus in Cana of Galilee, and manifested forth his glory; and *his disciples believed on him*" (2:11). The Lord Jesus had just influenced five men. John the Baptist had pointed him out, saying, "Behold, the Lamb of God" (John 1:29), and right away two of them followed Jesus. Simon, Philip, and then Nathanael followed him, but at first were puzzled as to his identity. Then they saw the glory of his presence, full of grace and truth, and the glory of his power, restoring order, releasing nature, reversing failure, and they looked at one another and said, "This is he of whom the prophets wrote; the Messiah indeed!" And they believed on him. So the glory of Christ's purpose is:

A. The Establishment of a Divine Relationship

"He came unto his own, and his own received him not. But as many as received him, to them gave he power to become the sons of God, even to them that believe on his name" (John 1:11-12). They believed on him, and the glory of the gospel was manifested in the establishment of a divine relationship. From that moment onward, those followers were the children of God by faith in him.

And so it is with us. We become the children of God by receiving the Lord Jesus and believing in him. That is more than believing *about* him. It is more than intellectual assent: it is heart consent. It is the commitment of the mind, heart, and will to Jesus Christ as Savior and Lord.

Illustration

A. T. Schofield, the Harley Street physician, was fifteen when he started school at a private academy in Rhyl, North Wales. When his new roommate inquired, "Are you a Christian?" Schofield replied that he was not, for, although he had been religiously brought up, his parents' teaching had fallen on deaf ears. Then his companion asked, "Would you like to be one?" A. T. Schofield replied, "It's no use liking. I know well I never shall be a Christian."

His young mentor went off to a prayer meeting to pray for the new boy, and on his return tumbled into bed and fell asleep. But A. T. Schofield could not rest, knowing that the lad who shared the room with him was all right and he was all wrong. He tossed in uneasy sleep till nearly 2:00 A.M., asking himself why he could not rest like the boy in the next bed. Suddenly there came to his mind the words, "Because you won't take it." He realized then that he was very sick with the sin disease when all the time the medicine to heal his disease was within reach. The remedy was true personal belief in Christ his Savior. To simply believe in the medicine would do him no good: *he must take it.* There and then he prayed from his heart, "O God, I take Thy Son, Jesus Christ, to be my Savior this night," and dropped off to sleep.

The next morning a teacher came and sat beside him, and said, "We prayed for you last night. I'm so sorry you are not a Christian." "But I am one," he said to the master and related how he received the Lord at two o'clock in the morning. In telling his story, Dr. Schofield then added, "I rushed out of the house, threw my cap into the air, and ran around the playground to let off, as it were, some of the steam."[5] Herein is the glory of the gospel!

B. The Experience of a Divine Fellowship

"Truly our fellowship is with the Father, and with his Son Jesus Christ" (1 John 1:3). From the moment those disciples believed in the Lord Jesus they were in his circle. They prayed together, lived together, slept together, talked together, traveled together, and worked miracles together: He, the leader and divine Son; and they, not only his children by faith, but his followers and friends (John 15:14).

Illustration

Among the Dutch, roses were sometimes cultivated by planting an inferior rose close to a rose of superior quality. The lesser rose was carefully watched, and its anthers removed to avoid self-pollinization and permit pollinization by the superior rose. Gradually the rose thus treated demonstrated the superior characteristics of its companion. This is indeed a beautiful illustration of the blessing that comes to the life that knows the companionship of Jesus. If our lives are pollinized, as it were, by his righteousness; if his life-transforming truth is received into the heart, if self is sacrificed to make room for the incoming of his superior life, it is inevitable that gradually the life will lose its own inferior characteristics and develop the characteristics of the blessed life of him who is himself the rose of Sharon.

It is wonderful to trace the development in the lives of the disciples from that day in Cana of Galilee through to the day of Pentecost. Truly, they were changed into his likeness, from glory to glory.

Do we know a fellowship like that in our lives? If not, we can have it, for it is all bound up in the glory of Christ as demonstrated in this miracle.

Conclusion

Jesus was called to the marriage and he came. We never hear of an invitation given to him which he refused. Have you invited him into your marriage, your home, your church, and, what is even more personal and relevant, have you invited him into your heart?

The Healing
of the Nobleman's Son:
Faith in Christ

4:43-54

Introduction

If the first miracle recorded in John's Gospel illustrates the glory of Christ the second miracle illustrates the reality of faith in Christ. It is interesting that there are three expressions in this story that relate to faith. Twice it is specifically stated that the nobleman "believed" (4:50, 53); and again, he "besought" Jesus (4:47). The word "besought" in the Greek is stronger than the words "to ask" or "to petition" and conveys the idea of "pleading in faith." These steps of faith illustrate the movements in the process of an individual's salvation. No one can be truly saved through faith in Christ alone until he has progressed through these three movements of faith.

I. The Creation of the Nobleman's Faith

"When he heard that Jesus was come out of Judea into Galilee, he went unto him, and besought him that he would come down, and heal his son: for he was at the point of death" (4:47). As we read through this story we notice the progression of this man's approach to Christ. First he heard, then he came, finally he sought. Christian faith grows from these three essentials.

A. He Heard of Christ

"When he heard that Jesus was come out of Judea into Galilee, he went unto him" (4:47). He had been told of the mighty work of Jesus and had come to understand that he was no ordinary person. Perhaps he even glimpsed, intellectually, that here was the Son of God, the Messiah, and he figured that if ever a miracle was going to be performed upon his son it would have to be done by this Jesus.

Many people ask why missionaries go out to the foreign field and disturb the culture, thinking, and practices of people of another nation. The man who understands the sovereignty of God in redemption, as revealed through all the followers of Jesus Christ, realizes that we are committed to a task of evangelism that knows no national barriers. "How then shall they call on him in whom they have not believed? and how shall they believe in him of whom they have not heard? and how shall they hear without a preacher? . . . So then faith cometh by hearing, and hearing by the word of God" (Rom. 10:14, 17). A more literal translation would be, "Faith cometh by hearing, and hearing by the gospel of Christ."

B. He Came to Christ

"When he heard that Jesus was come out of Judea into Galilee, he went [came] unto him" (4:47). When faith is created in the human heart by the Word of God, there is a movement toward Christ. Inertia is replaced by action, the voluntary response of the mind, heart, and will.

Many people imagine that they can drift into an experience of Christ when the appropriate but undefined time arrives, but this is a delusion. There is nothing fortuitous about a personal confrontation with Jesus Christ. Christianity is not "the opiate of the people," it is rather a deliberate choice, a rational and responsible encounter with the Son of God. The Lord Jesus made this very clear when he preached the gospel of the kingdom. To some he said, *"Come* unto me" (Matt. 11:28); to others he commanded *"Follow* me" (Luke 9:23), and to those who tended to hesitate he urged *"Strive* [or "agonize"] to enter in at the strait gate" (Luke 13:24)—all active verbs that call for a vigorous response.

C. He Asked of Christ

He "besought him that he would come . . . and heal his son" (4:47). The word "besought" means "asked," "besieged," "desired," "entreated," or "prayed." We have made this whole matter of salvation so cheap and easy that people have forgotten the great travail of soul through which men and women in past generations have had to go in order to come to Christ. The modern generation sits passively in church and expects the Lord to come and do them a favor. True salvation from sin demands of us a deep, heart exercise. God wants to see this earnestness in terms of repentance, faith, and obedience. We know that salvation is "not of works, lest any man should boast" (Eph. 2:9), but at the same time it is an active, appropriating faith.

Illustration

In order to clarify what faith involved, C. H. Spurgeon used to employ this illustration. Suppose there is a fire on the third floor of a house, and a child is trapped in a room

there. A huge, strong man stands on the ground beneath
the window where the child's face appears, and he calls
"Jump!" "It is a part of faith," Spurgeon would say, "to
know that there is a man there; still another part of faith
to believe him to be a strong man; but the essence of
faith lies in trusting him fully and dropping into his arms."
Thus it is with the sinner and Christ.[1]

II. The Conviction of the Nobleman's Faith

"Then said Jesus unto him, Except ye see signs and
wonders, ye will not believe" (4:48). Though the nobleman was in anguish and tears, the Lord did not spare him.
He had to believe first, and *then* see the touch of healing
upon his son. Two demands were made upon his faith:

A. Obedience to the Word

"Go thy way; thy son liveth. And the man believed
the word that Jesus had spoken unto him, and he went
his way" (4:50). The conviction of faith which follows
the creation of faith will come when there is obedience
to the Word. Paul had this in mind when he wrote the
Epistle to the Romans and talked about "the obedience
of faith" (Rom. 16:26). James implied it when he wrote,
"Faith without works is dead" (James 2:26). Dietrich
Bonhoeffer, in his book, *The Cost of Discipleship,*
writes: "Faith is not faith unless it leads to obedience."
Jesus said to this nobleman, "Go thy way; thy son
liveth. And the man believed the word that Jesus had
spoken unto him, and he went his way" (4:50).

There is no substitute for obedience, either in sinner
or saint, for as we have seen already, faith that does not
lead to obedience is not faith at all.

Illustration

Through United Press comes the report that termites
have eaten through a large stack of pamphlets entitled,
Control of Termites, in the mailing room of the University

of California at Berkeley. It is one thing to have in a pamphlet the information concerning the control of termites, and quite another thing to make a practical application of that information! On speaking to His disciples on one occasion, the Lord Jesus said regarding the things He taught them, *"If ye know these things, happy are ye if ye do them"* (John 13:7).[2]

B. Dependence on the Lord

He "himself believed, and his whole house" (4:53). When the man discovered that his son had been healed it affected not only his own life, but that of his entire household. As we shall see in a moment, he became an open follower of the Lord Jesus. From that moment on he lived by faith and not by sight. He had learned the lesson that Thomas needed to learn after the resurrection, when he insisted, "Except I shall see in his hands the print of the nails, and put my finger into the print of the nails, and thrust my hand into his side, I will not believe" (John 20:25). Jesus had to say to him, "Blessed are they that have not seen, and yet have believed" (John 20:29). This is the message that Habakkuk, Paul, and Martin Luther preached, namely, "The just shall live by faith" (Hab. 2:4; Rom. 1:17).

Illustration

Martin Luther, as a monk, "happened on a volume of the Scriptures. He knew it only as a forbidden book. He read it furtively until he came to the place where it is written, 'There is none other name under heaven given among men, whereby we must be saved.' He read, 'By the deeds of the law there shall no flesh be justified. . . . What the law could not do, in that it was weak through the flesh, God sending his own Son. . . .' The light began to break. He [went] to Rome. He determined on penance by climbing . . . the Sacred Stairway on his knees. Half way up he seemed to hear a voice saying, 'The just shall live by faith!' and the day broke. He stood erect, a believer in Christ as his only Savior from sin."[3]

III. The Confession of the Nobleman's Faith

"So the father knew that it was at the same hour, in the which Jesus said unto him, Thy son liveth: and himself believed, and his whole house" (4:53). The Bible teaches that the Christian faith is a confessional faith. Christ never called for secret disciples. This explains why the early Christians were publicly baptized right after their conversion. Baptism is the outward expression of an inward experience of personal faith in Christ. The confession of faith has a twofold aspect:

A. *Confession to God*

"That if thou shalt confess with thy mouth the Lord Jesus, and shalt believe in thine heart that God hath raised him from the dead, thou shalt be saved" (Rom. 10:9); and again: "For whosoever shall call upon the name of the Lord shall be saved" (Rom. 10:13). Somewhere along that long journey (25 miles) to his home, the nobleman must have committed himself to the Lord Jesus Christ in an act of faith. And this is how it should be. Anything less than this is hypocritical and unreal. We cannot confess outwardly what we do not know inwardly of personal faith in Jesus Christ.

B. *Confession to Men*

"So the father knew that it was at the same hour, in the which Jesus said unto him, Thy son liveth: and himself believed, and his whole house" (4:53). So real was this man's experience of faith in Christ that he was able to influence his whole household. His confession to God was matched by his confession to men—and this is how it should be. The Lord Jesus said, "Whosoever therefore shall confess me before men, him will I confess also before my Father which is in heaven" (Matt. 10:32).

On the day of Pentecost we see this twofold confession dramatically exemplified. After Peter had preached his God-anointed sermon there was, first of all, *conviction of sin*. The hearers cried out, "Men and brethren, what shall we do?" (Acts 2:37). Then followed *conversion of life*. Peter said, "Repent, and be baptized every one of you in the name of Jesus Christ for the remission of sins" (Acts 2:38), and that issued in *confession of faith*—"They that gladly received his word were baptized: and the same day there were added unto them about three thousand souls" (Acts 2:41). This demonstration of enthusiastic faith is the evidence of the genuine working of God in the human soul.

Illustration

Henry J. Heinz, of the fifty-seven varieties fame, wrote his will as follows: "Looking forward to the time when my earthly career will end, I desire to set forth at the very beginning of this will, as the most important item in it, a confession of my faith in Jesus Christ as my Saviour. I also desire to bear witness to the fact that throughout my life, in which were the usual joys and sorrows, I have been wonderfully sustained by my faith in God through Jesus Christ. This legacy was left me by my consecrated mother, a woman of strong faith, and to it I attribute any success I have attained."[4]

Conclusion

This living miracle of the healing of the nobleman's son has taught us an important lesson about faith in Christ. We have seen what is meant by the creation of faith, the conviction of faith, and the confession of faith. Where true faith is born in a person's life he is never apologetic. On the contrary, his walk and talk reflect joy and confidence. Faith is to believe what we do not see; and the reward of this faith is to see what we believe.

10

The Making Whole
of a Crippled Life:
The Complete Cure

5:1-15; 7:23

Introduction

Here is a story which beautifully illustrates the completeness of the cure which the Lord Jesus can effect in the lives of men and women who are afflicted by the disease of sin. The setting for this event was the city of Jerusalem at the time of "the feast" (some manuscripts include the article *he*—"the first") which would naturally mean the Passover; but there is no way of being certain what feast it was that Jesus attended here. Ever aware of the needy souls around him, he made his way to the pool of Bethesda, near the sheep market. The name means "the house of mercy," and there lay a great multitude of sick people—blind, crippled and withered. Among the most desperate of all was a man who had been an invalid for thirty-eight years. Time and again, he had tried to avail himself of the healing waters bubbling up from an underground spring, but without success. Disappointed and frustrated, he lay there, unable to move. Then the Lord Jesus appeared on the scene and spoke words which instantly brought about a complete cure.

I. The Word of Divine Diagnosis

"Wilt thou be made whole?" (5:6). "Do you know what is really wrong with you? Do you want to be rid of this complaint?" he asked. The piercing eyes of the Lord Jesus had looked beyond the external, and by his question he brought home to the man's heart just what his condition was. The words that the Savior spoke revealed:

A. The Health He Needed

"Jesus saw him lie, and knew that he had been now a long time in that case" (5:6). Sin ultimately affects physical health, and Jesus Christ coupled this man's malady with his sinful life. "Sin no more, lest a worse thing come unto thee" (5:14), were his parting words to him.

And this is true of men and women today. However fit they may appear to be at the moment, if they refuse the complete cure which is available in Jesus Christ, sin will bring them to the place of ultimate ill health—death (1 Cor. 11:30).

Illustration

"Sin" really does exist, according to Dr. Karl Menninger. The famous psychiatrist is distressed that modern society tries to figure out its problems and talk about morality without ever mentioning the word "sin." He is convinced that the only way to raise the moral tone of present-day civilization and deal with the depression and worries that plague clergy, psychiatrists, and ordinary folk is to revive an understanding of what "sin" is.[1]

B. The Help He Needed

"Sir, I have no man, when the water is troubled, to put me into the pool" (5:7). Sin affects not only the physical, but the social life. Here was someone who was alone and lonely. No one would pity him or help him. Perhaps his manner of sinful living had turned even his best friends against him. Like the psalmist, he had to cry, "No man cared for my soul" (Ps. 142:4).

The Scriptures show that though there is a confederacy of sin, the time comes when sin separates even worldly friends from each other.

Illustration

Cite the story of the prodigal son (Luke 15:11-32), and emphasize the words "and no man gave unto him" (v. 16).

C. The Hope He Needed

"Sir, I have no man, when the water is troubled, to put me into the pool: but while I am coming, another steppeth down before me" (5:7). He had lost all hope. And the Bible speaks of men and women "having no hope, and without God in the world" (Eph. 2:12).

Sin affects the physical, social and the spiritual realms of the human personality. This man had a diseased body, a defiled soul, and a dead spirit. In theological terms, we speak of man's "total depravity"; and by that we mean that sin has invaded the entire being. It is no wonder, then, that Jesus addressed him with the words, "Wilt thou be made whole?" (5:6). Jesus said, "They that be whole need not a physician, but they that are sick" (Matt. 9:12).

Exegesis

It is important to point out that verse 4 is missing in the oldest and best manuscripts. In all probability it was added, like the clause in verse 3, to make clear the statement in verse 7. The Jews explained the healing virtue of the intermittent springs by attributing it to the ministry of angels.

Illustration

Dr. Walter Wilson, ever on the alert to speak to men about their souls and need of the Saviour, asked an attendant at a service station who had filled his car with gas: "How did sin get in Sinclair?" pointing to the lighted sign atop the gas pump. "I do not know, sir, how sin got into Sinclair; but, sir, I have wished many times that I knew how to get sin out of my life!" It was then that Dr. Wilson had the opportunity to tell the young man of the One who is the sinner's friend and of whom it is written: "And thou shalt call his name Jesus: for he shall save his people from their sins" (Matt. 1:21).[2]

II. The Word of Divine Deliverance

"Rise, take up thy bed, and walk" (5:8), were the Savior's words. And the man realized that he was in the presence of one whose eyes shone with the glory of heaven, and who spoke with the voice of authority. Such was the redemptive power of the word spoken that a threefold deliverance took place in this man's life:

A. A Spiritual Deliverance

"Rise" (5:8). This was the word which quickened his dead spirit; and the Lord Jesus always starts with the spirit. Later he could say to him, "Behold, thou art made . . . [well]: sin no more, lest a worse thing come unto thee" (5:14). Writing to the Ephesians, Paul could say, "You hath he quickened, who were dead in trespasses and sins" (Eph. 2:1). This is the nature of spiritual deliverance. It involves not only the remission of past sins, but the regeneration of our spirits; a mighty deliverance indeed!

Illustration

When the lame man and the healing pool and the Master came together, there was health and hope. When the little lad and the few loaves and fishes and the Master came together, there was sufficiency and even abundance. A thirsty woman, an ancient well, and the Master, and there were streams of living water flowing into human hearts. A rugged fisherman, a broken net, and the Master, and there was discipleship, and a story to tell. Wherever a human need and a sincere faith and the Master meet, there is transformation and consecration. If we bring our lives, weak and insufficient, to the Master, He will remake us.[3]

B. A Moral Deliverance

"Take up thy bed" (5:8). At that command the man rolled it up and put it on his shoulder. Someone has said that he did this in order to show that he was making no provision for a relapse!

It may be that you have been laid low by temptation again and again. You may have tried discipline and reformation, but without the delivering word of Jesus Christ you will never know moral deliverance.

It is a wonderful day when we can pick up and carry away the very thing that symbolizes our moral defeat. Observe that this man had the courage to carry his pallet (the bed of the very poor), even on the Sabbath day. Carrying furniture on the Sabbath was the kind of work prohibited by the rabbis in their strict interpretation of the fourth commandment. When we know the deliverance of Christ we fear no one but God.

Illustration

A painter once painted the devil playing a game of chess with a young man whose eternal soul was at stake. The scene showed the devil with a look of glee on his face as he checkmates the young man whose look of despair acknowledges defeat. There appears no other move for him to make. A great chess player came across the work of art and, after carefully studying the game, he set up a chess board with the pieces in a similar position. After much thought and time, he saw that defeat could be turned into victory. By making just one certain move on the young man's behalf, the devil was placed in a position of utter defeat.

In the game of life, youth has no chance against the wiles of the devil who is determined to ruin the soul. But at Calvary the Lord Jesus intervened and made a "move" that enables [all] who trust [him] to have complete victory. "Thanks be unto God who giveth us the victory through our Lord Jesus Christ."[4]

C. A Physical Deliverance

"Rise, take up thy bed, and *walk*" (5:8). New life was flowing through him as he walked through the streets of Jerusalem that day. And it is God's will for us, apart from the mystery of suffering, that we should be quickened in our mortal bodies, and glow with abundant life and vigor. One day we shall have perfect, incorruptible bodies, like our Lord's. In the meantime, however, God intends that we should know his supernatural strength, even when we are weak. The apostle Paul knew something of this during his life and ministry. Even though afflicted by a thorn in the flesh, he could rejoice in his many afflictions, and declare, "When I am weak, then am I strong" (2 Cor. 12:10).

Exegesis

"Rise, take up thy bed, and walk" (John 5:8). Notice that the present active imperative of *egeirō* is a sort of exclamation like our "get up!" The first active imperative (*āron* or *airō*) means "to pick up the pallet and go on walking." This present continuous verb underscores the magnitude of deliverance which Jesus can effect in our lives.

III. The Word of Divine Direction

"Afterward Jesus findeth him in the temple, and said unto him, Behold, thou art made whole: sin no more, lest a worse thing come unto thee" (5:14). Observe that it is in the temple that Jesus gives divine direction. That is why the church exists, not for the world but for the family of God. The world is to be evangelized by an outgoing church. The church is the hospital for the sick, the home for the lonely, and the school for the uninstructed in the family of God. Jesus found this man in the temple and told him to do three things:

A. Live a Life of Radiant Certainty

"Afterward Jesus findeth him in the temple, and said unto him, Behold, thou art made whole" (5:14). This is the first thing we should teach those who have recently come to Christ. One of the devices of the devil is to rob us of radiant certainty. John could write to his converts and say, "These things have I written unto you that believe on the name of the Son of God; that ye may know that ye have eternal life" (1 John 5:13).

When God says to us, "You are made whole," it is not something to question, or even debate; it is something to believe and rejoice in. So many Christians lose their joy because they become morbidly introspective. C. H. Spurgeon warned against this when he said, "I looked to Jesus, and the dove of peace came into my soul; I looked at the dove and it flew away." The secret of certainty is keeping our eyes on Jesus.

Illustration

At a certain church a boy of ten years of age was examined for membership. After he had spoken of his sense of guilt, came the question, "What did you do when you felt yourself so great a sinner?" and the eyes of the boy brightened as he answered, "I just went to Jesus and told Him how sinful I was, and how sorry I was, and asked Him to forgive me." "And do you hope at times that Jesus heard you and forgave your sins?" "I don't only hope so, sir, I know He did." "How do you know it, my son?" Every eye was intent on the little respondent. "He said He would," said the boy, with a look of astonishment, as if amazed that anyone should doubt it.[5]

B. Live a Life of Radiant Victory

"Sin no more" (5:14). Jesus would never have said such a thing to tantalize a man if it were not possible. Jesus not only gives the command, but also the enabling. And we have promises to support this glorious truth: "For sin shall not have dominion over you: for ye are not under the law, but under grace" (Rom. 6:14); "Thanks be unto God, which always causeth us to triumph in Christ" (2 Cor. 2:14); "In all these things we are more than conquerors through him that loved us" (Rom. 8:37). Someone has said that the victorious Christian life is the victorious Christ in us.

Illustration

Hudson Taylor at thirty-seven, already a mighty man of faith and a great missionary warrior, was longing for a victory he did not have. He was often restless and irritated, defeated in his prayer life, a struggling Christian, wondering if there was not something better for him. He read a letter from a fellow missionary of the China Inland Mission, one little known, who told his director out of a full heart how he had come into joy and peace and victory. Hudson Taylor "saw it in a flash," he writes, and his "exchanged life" began: the miracle of Christ working out through him.[6]

C. Live a Life of Radiant Loyalty

"Sin no more, lest a worse thing come unto thee" (5:14). The life of faith is a life of utter dependence on the Lord Jesus to do in and through us what we cannot achieve of ourselves. God ordained it that way to teach us that there is only one place of victory, and that is in Christ. Peter could walk on the water while he kept his eyes on his master, but the moment he looked at the boisterous waves he began to sink.

Loyalty means following the Lord Jesus in undeviating obedience and steadfast love. When the Lord Jesus said, "Sin no more, lest a worse thing come unto thee" (5:14), he was issuing a serious warning. To fail at this point in his life was to invite a worse disaster than the thirty-eight years of illness from which he had been just delivered! He would now be sinning against the light that he had just received. Loyalty is not optional, in the life of a Christian: it is obligatory, if we are to please our Savior and to enjoy the fullness of his blessing.

Illustration

A magnificent monument was erected in England soon after the close of World War II and was dedicated to the memory of three women who had served their country as secret agents at the cost of their lives. One of them had been terribly tortured by the enemy before her death, as they sought to obtain information that was locked away in her mind. Misunderstood, hated by their own countrymen, their lives in constant hazard, the noble three had gone on until each in turn was apprehended and put to death, with honor coming to them posthumously, driven on by their noble sense of loyalty that was a fundamental part of their characters. "Be thou faithful unto death, and I will give thee a crown of life" (Rev. 2:10).[7]

Conclusion

We have studied together a story which illustrates the Savior's power to cure completely. The Lord Jesus never does things by halves; he always goes all the way. His is not only the double cure, it is the triple cure: He heals the spirit, soul, and body. Let our prayer be:

> Out of my bondage, sorrow and night,
> Jesus, I come, Jesus, I come;
> Into Thy freedom, gladness, and light,
> Jesus, I come to Thee;
> Out of my sickness into Thy health,
> Out of my want and into Thy wealth,
> Out of my sin and into Thyself,
> Jesus, I come to Thee.
> William T. Sleeper

11

The Feeding of the
Five Thousand:
The Satisfying Savior

6:1-14

Introduction

One of the fascinating features of Christ's earthly ministry was his way with crowds of people. Over and over again we find him followed by multitudes, or speaking to multitudes.

It is true, of course, that the salvation experience is an individual encounter; God does not save people en masse—even though the history of evangelism and missions shows that vast numbers have turned to Christ in times of revival. People enter the kingdom one by one, yet Christ also appeals to the crowds. The phenomenon of mass evangelism in the past, and in modern times, more than substantiates this.

In the story before us, we have an outstanding illustration of our subject. The feeding of the five thousand is recorded in each of the four Gospels (Matt. 14:13-21; Mark 6:30-44; Luke 9:10-17; John 6:1-13). It is well to read each of the accounts in order to get the full picture; but the main points we want to make are clearly here in the passage before us.

I. The Crowd Saw the Attraction of Christ

"A great multitude followed him" (6:2). There was something about the Lord Jesus which attracted people. Mark has a beautiful line in his record which reads, "They came to him [the Lord Jesus] from every quarter" (Mark 1:45). Even though his enemies, the Jewish leaders, despised him and eventually rejected him, they could not stop the common people from converging on him whenever they had an opportunity. As we study the Gospels, we see three things that created this attraction in Christ:

A. Christ's Magnetism

"The people . . . followed him: and he received them" (Luke 9:11). A little child's reaction to a person is a good test of that person's character. This was particularly true of the Lord Jesus. Children loved to run into his arms. This is why the master had to rebuke his disciples when they attempted to shield him from the "intrusion" of little ones.

Even sinners found it easy to come to him and tell him their problems and seek his help. This attraction to Christ was evident in the case of individuals, as well as the multitudes. In him people saw the irresistible qualities of grace and truth; hearts responded to the grace, with its warmth, and truth, with its strength—and that is still true today. Jesus prophesied: "And I, if I be lifted up from the earth, will draw all men unto me" (John 12:32).

Illustration

A man's life is always more forcible than his speech; when men take stock of him they reckon his deeds as [dollars] and his words as [cents]. If his life and his doctrine disagree the mass of lookers-on accept his practice and reject his preaching.[1]

Illustration

Stephen Olford recounts how he was once asked to explain Billy Graham's magnetism. He said that there were three qualities which attracted people. First, he is a man with charisma. When the anointing of the Spirit is upon a man, God gives him an acceptance among the people. Second, he is a man of courage. All over the world he is known as a preacher who punctuates every sermon with the words, "The Bible says." Even in a day when the authority of the Word of God is being challenged, people long to hear a man speak with authority. Third, he is a man of compassion. Even his critics admit that he really cares for people. He proved this in the days of the civil rights struggle as well as his visits to disaster areas of the world and his concern for social injustice today. Like his master, he exudes both truth and grace, and this is what makes him a magnetic personality.

B. Christ's Message

"The people . . . followed him: and he received them, and spake unto them of the kingdom of God" (Luke 9:11). People have always flocked to listen to a man with a real message. And such was the significance, authority, and challenge of the Savior's words that the people—great or small, simple or educated—thronged him. They discerned the difference between him and the scribes and Pharisees, and "wondered at the gracious words which proceeded out of his mouth" (Luke 4:22). On one occasion, when soldiers were sent to apprehend him, they turned and went back; and when asked for a reason their reply was, "Never man spake like this man" (John 7:46). Here was a man who had something to say, and he said it with such authority that it "rang a bell" in the souls of men and women. They knew instinctively that this was a word from heaven, something which could not be denied.

Illustration

If preachers insist on competing with psychiatrists as counselors, with physicians as healers, with politicians as statesmen and with philosophers as speculators, then these specialists have every right to tell them how to preach. If a minister's message is not based on "Thus saith the Lord," then as a sermon it is good for nothing but to be cast out and trodden under foot of the specialists in the department with which it deals.[2]

C. Christ's Miracles

"A great multitude followed him, because they saw his miracles which he did on them that were diseased" (6:2). Here was one who not only spoke, but acted. Had his ministry ended with his words he would have ultimately lost his audience, for most people are shrewd enough to discard preaching that doesn't result in practicing. That is why our politicians are constantly challenged about their campaign promises with the verbal barb, "All smoke and no fire."

Our Savior, however, was known not only for what he said, but what he did. A great theologian came to meet him one night. Looking into his face, he said, Master, "we know that thou art a teacher come from God: for no man can do these miracles that thou doest, except God be with him" (John 3:2). In other words, he was saying, "There is authority not only in your message, but in your miracles."

II. The Crowd Sensed the Compassion of Christ

"Jesus then lifted up his eyes, and saw a great company come unto him" (6:5). We read in Matthew and

Mark that when Jesus saw the multitude he was moved with compassion. That word "compassion" means "to enter into another's deep anguish," "to feel sympathy," "to have pity." One authority has pointed out that it conveys the idea of "getting into the skin of another." This is the way the Lord Jesus felt about individuals and multitudes.

A. His Compassion Was Born of Vision

"Jesus then lifted up his eyes, and saw a great company come unto him" (6:5). Here was one who saw men and women as no one else saw them.

There is a type of man who sees a crowd of people in terms of population. He thinks only of their numerical strength. Another type looks at a large group and counts them as hands. He thinks in terms of the labor force. And there is yet another whose first thought is that of popularity: "I must be something when a crowd like this comes along to see me!" He thinks in terms of status.

But very few men today, outside of those who know the compassion of Jesus Christ, look upon people as he saw them. When he lifted up his eyes he saw them not so much as a crowd, but as individuals.

Illustration

The story is told of C. H. Spurgeon, who was billed to speak at the Crystal Palace. He went ahead of time to test out his voice and the hall's acoustics. Standing on the rostrum, in what he thought was a great empty auditorium, he quoted John 3:16: "For God so loved the world, that he gave his only begotten Son, that whosoever believeth in him should not perish, but have everlasting life." A workman hidden behind the platform (indeed, still erecting part of it) heard the words and was saved on the spot. When Spurgeon came back later that day to address the crowd, thirty thousand people had gathered, and as he stood up to speak, he had to pause and compose himself, so moved was he with the sight of those people.

B. His Compassion Was Born of Passion

"Jesus, when he came out, saw much people, and was moved with compassion toward them" (Mark 6:34). Jeremiah says, "Mine eye affecteth mine heart" (Lam. 3:51). A person who really sees human need *feels* human need. The multitudes who followed him recognized that Jesus not only saw them, but loved them. His heart went out to them in tenderness.

Illustrations

Among the first glimpses we get of our God is that of a Seeker: "Adam . . . Where art thou?" (Gen. 3:9). In commenting upon this question, a teacher said, "You can never be a preacher if you read it as though God were a policeman. Read it as though God were a brokenhearted Father looking for a lost child!"[3]

Great sermons begin in great hearts, and hearts are made great by tilling them with the needs of a brokenhearted, suffering world. Jesus' trained ears could hear a beggar's cry above the shouts of the throng.[4]

III. The Crowd Shared the Provision of Christ

"When Jesus then lifted up his eyes, and saw a great company come unto him, he saith unto Philip, Whence shall we buy bread, that these may eat?" (6:5). In Matthew, Mark, and Luke, Jesus said, "Give ye them to eat" (Matt. 14:16, Mark 6:37, Luke 9:13). How these words spell out not only the redemptive compassion of Christ, but his practical concern for men and women. After all, the master had taken time with his disciples for refreshment and fellowship. Why should he bother with the thronging crowds at this time? Surely, they could wait for a more appropriate occasion. But that was not how Jesus thought. His compassion led him to action, and so we read of:

A. A Merciful Provision

"Whence shall we buy bread, that these may eat?" (6:5). These people had seen the Lord Jesus leading his disciples away to a solitary place across the lake for a time of relaxation and rest, a time to recapture true perspectives. The people outraced Jesus and his disciples and arrived before the ship reached the other side. There were at least five thousand men, women, and children, and they were tired and hungry. The disciples did not appear to have observed this, but Jesus made a thoughtful provision. Looking upon the multitude, he said to Philip, "We must feed this crowd. Whence shall we buy bread?" Philip, the "mathematician," began to work it out in terms of two hundred pennyworth, but what was that among so many? Then Andrew pointed out that there was a lad with a few loaves and fishes, but how could they ever be stretched to feed such a crowd? Jesus himself knew what he would do, and in his provision there was forethought and faithfulness.

Illustration

A theological student came to Charles Spurgeon one day, greatly concerned that he could not grasp the meaning of certain verses in the Bible. The noted preacher replied kindly but firmly, "Young man, allow me to give you this word of advice. Give the Lord credit for knowing things you don't understand."[5]

B. A Multiplied Provision

"Jesus took the loaves; and when he had given thanks, he distributed to the disciples, and the disciples to them that were set down; and likewise of the fishes as much as they would" (6:11). There is something profound and beautiful here. What has the Lord Jesus Christ done? He has taken into his holy hands the simple barley loaves and sardines from the little boy. Barley loaves were the food of the simplest and poorest people of the community. The rich man gave barley loaves to his horse, or mule, or ass.

The miracle here is not that of speeding up the processes of nature, as when the water was made into wine. Rather, it is based on the principle that what is good or sufficient for one is sufficient for all. If there were only one sinner in the whole world, he would still require the death of the Son of God at Calvary's cross. And what was food for one healthy boy was food good enough for everyone, in the master's hands.

The Lord Jesus taking those five barley loaves in his hands illustrates the work of redemption. When he came from heaven he did not take the nature of angels, but was made in the likeness of men. He was incarnated in the simple material of human clay, and through it effected redemption. And in taking upon him humanity, he came as a little babe, born in a manger, to become the Savior of the world. Jesus took an insignificant boy in the crowd and made him the instrument of feeding five thousand. Taking the loaves into his hands, he gave thanks before distributing them. That was the Eucharist, the same thanksgiving as he uttered when he broke the bread to represent his broken body. It was a picture of Calvary, when the miracle of multiplication by subtraction began and has gone on ever since. Although there is only one Christ, he dwells in millions of people now.

Illustration

The story was told in the *Christian Herald* of a teacher in London, an unbeliever, who was telling her class the story of the five loaves and two fishes and trying to explain away the miracle in the account. "Of course you will understand, children, that it does not actually mean that Jesus fed all those people with such a small amount of food. That would be impossible. It means that He fed the people with His teaching, so that they lost all sense of bodily hunger and went home satisfied." But one little girl, not satisfied with that teaching asked, "But, teacher, what was it that filled the twelve baskets afterward, if it wasn't really food?" Good logic, and good faith![6]

C. A Ministered Provision

"Jesus said, Make the men sit down. . . . And Jesus took the loaves; and when he had given thanks, he distributed" (6:10-11). They had to sit down and wait to be ministered to.

And the Lord Jesus Christ insists upon that today. Remember he has said: "I am the bread of life: he that cometh to me shall never hunger; and he that believeth on me shall never thirst" (John 6:35). If he would be your minister of this Bread of Life, he would condition you for two things: first, *to believe the blesser.* These people were conditioned for that. Their eyes were focused on him. They saw in the Lord Jesus such authority and sufficiency, and such a promise of blessing, that they believed. Secondly, they sat down ready *to receive the blessing,* and then the multiplication began. Through his disciples he ministered to them the bread and the fishes, and when they had eaten and were filled, we read that there were twelve baskets full of fragments. Such was the multiplied and ministered provision from the Savior's hands.

Amplification

Show that Christ met not only the needs of the multitude, but also of his disciples. Notice John 6:13, "They . . . filled twelve baskets with the fragments." Some have suggested that it was one basket for each of the apostles, but without doubt the lad had his share as well. God never gives sparingly.

Conclusion

Few passages of the Word of God could be more relevant to our day. We live in a world of unbelievable starvation and privation. There are countries such as the Far East and Africa where people are literally dying by the thousands each day. What is the church doing about this?

We have seen Christ's way with the crowds, and we have learned of an attraction, a compassion, and a provision which are so characteristic of our God. Is that same Savior living and working in and through us? What do people see, sense, or share when we minister to them? Remember that the master still says today, as he said then, "Give ye them to eat" (Matt. 14:16).

12

The Walking on the Water:
The Christ of Today
6:16-21

Introduction

It is one of the sad features of modern preaching that so often the emphasis is placed entirely upon the Jesus of history. Stories such as this are used merely as lessons, and we are exhorted to imitate, in our own strength (or weakness) the Jesus of history who touched the heads of little children, fed the hungry, healed the leper, and caused the blind to see.

Such a doctrine, however, is not the teaching of the New Testament concerning the Christ of today, the Christ of Christianity. The apostle Paul clearly states in his second Epistle to the Corinthians: "Though we have known Christ after the flesh, yet now henceforth know we him no more" (2 Cor. 5:16). Why? Because he is no longer merely the Jesus of history. He is the risen Christ, the Lord of glory. His significance for us today lies not simply in the facts of his life and death in Palestine, though those are historic facts upon which our faith is based. The relevance of God in Christ for a world of today is that Jesus lives, and is operative in the everyday world in which we find ourselves. This beautiful story helps to elucidate the ever-present ministry of the risen Christ. We have here three pictures of him. See him, first of all, as:

I. The Christ of Sympathy

"He departed . . . into a mountain himself alone" (6:15). John does not include the words "to pray," but Matthew does (14:23). Events that had just transpired were burdening the heart of the Lord Jesus, and he must take them to the place of prayer, the place of advantage, from whence he could intercede and intervene. John the Baptist had just been beheaded. Jesus had shared this news with the disciples, who were depressed beyond measure. That is why they took to the boat on the lake and spent a whole day there. The sight of the multitude, too, had made his heart heavy, for they were as sheep without a shepherd, confused and without direction or care. So the Savior had ministered to them in healing, preaching and feeding. Again, the Lord Jesus was burdened as he looked upon his disciples. So often they disappointed him when they did not rise to the occasion. They wanted to send that hungry multitude away. Now they are on the lake. A storm has blown up, and they are toiling in rowing. The heart of the Savior goes out to them as he watched them, for he is the Christ of sympathy.

What happened historically, then, is, in fact, true today. The Christ of sympathy has ascended the mountain to the throne, where he shares all our experiences. "We have not an high priest which cannot be touched with the feeling of our infirmities; but was in all points tempted like as we are, yet without sin" (Heb. 4:15). There is no heartthrob or experience of life here upon earth that he does not feel from his throne.

A. His Place of Intercession

"Wherefore he is able also to save them to the uttermost that come unto God by him, seeing he ever liveth to make intercession for them" (Heb. 7:25). Someone may be saying, "I have no mother, father, Sunday school teacher, to pray for me," but there is one who is praying for you now. He is the one who, on that mountaintop that day, prayed for the vast multitude who wended their way into the darkness, to camp out, or to reach the villages beyond. He prayed, too, for his anxious disciples as they struggled against wind and tide: "Father, strengthen them; let not their faith fail; impress upon them the great truths I have sought to inculcate."

B. His Place of Intervention

"Whosoever shall call upon the name of the Lord shall be saved" (Rom. 10:13). From his vantage point the Lord Jesus could see the plight of his disciples, and move to their aid. Seasoned fishermen though they were, they were unable to cope with the great storm that had blown up. They had reached the point of no return, halfway across the lake; a dangerous and frightening position to be in. It was in such a state that Jesus saw his disciples and came to their rescue.

So, today, from his vantage point, the sympathetic Savior sees and knows all about us, and swiftly comes to our aid. The omniscient, omnipresent, and omnipotent Christ can touch the world at any and every point from his throne in heaven. His ear is ever open to our cry, and his arm ready and able to save.

Illustration

Visitors to the famous Gallery in St. Paul's Cathedral, London, can hear a whisper travel around the whole dome, the sound bouncing back many times from the smooth walls.

A number of years ago, a poor shoemaker whispered to his young lady that he could not afford to marry her as he hadn't money enough to buy any leather, and his business was ruined. The poor girl wept quietly as she listened to this sad news.

A gentleman on the other side of the gallery, which is 198 feet across, heard this story and the shoemaker's whispered prayer, and he decided to do something about it. After finding out where he lived, the gentleman had some leather sent along to the shop. Imagine how delighted the poor man was! He made good use of this gift, and his business prospered so that he was able to marry the girl of his choice. It was not till a few years later that he learned the name of his unknown friend—the Prime Minister of Great Britain, W. E. Gladstone.

There is always one above who hears our whispered sorrowings and prayers, and will take action. No matter how low we whisper he can hear. We cannot always tell our human friends about things, but God always knows, so we can tell him all in prayer, and he will hear and answer.[1]

II. The Christ of Victory

"They see Jesus walking on the sea, and drawing nigh unto the ship" (6:19). It was about six miles across the lake, so assuming that their fishing boat was halfway across ("in the midst of the sea" Mark 6:47), they were in a perilous position. Their boat might sink. To swim meant that they would have to cover some three miles—almost impossible in such a storm. This was indeed a crisis hour for that little group of men, but not for the Christ of victory. Consider, then:

A. *His Moment of Victory*

"And in the fourth watch of the night Jesus went unto them, walking on the sea" (Matt. 14:25). It was psychologically planned; not before or after time, but just at the moment of desperate need. God knows just when to move into a person's experience.

Matthew and Mark tell us that Jesus came to his disciples "in the fourth watch of the night," which is the darkest hour before dawn. Focus on that concept throughout the Scriptures. Think of the four hundred years of darkness before Jesus was born. Think of the delay prior to the death of Lazarus. Think of the timing before the rescue of the storm-tossed disciples. There is a point at which he must intervene—and it is always the right moment.

Illustration

Aquilla Webb asked a lifeguard at Newport, Rhode Island: "How can you tell when anyone is in need of help when there are thousands of bathers on the beach and in the water making a perfect hub-bub of noises?" He answered: "No matter how great the noise and confusion, there has never been a single time when I could not distinguish the cry of distress above them all. I can always tell it." Webb comments, "That is exactly like God. In the midst of the babel and confusion he never fails to hear the soul that cries out to him for help amid the breakers and storms of life."[2]

B. His Manner of Victory

"They see Jesus walking on the sea" (6:19). Bishop Dodderidge pointed out that in Egyptian hieroglyphics, the sign of two feet upon water is the symbol of sovereign power. The "Jesus of history" that our radical friends talk about is limited, but the Jesus of authentic Christianity is the Christ of sovereignty, the master of the elements. There is no situation over which he is not triumphant. He muzzles the winds and says to the angry waves, "Be still," and they obey.

The Christ of victory is equal to anything that threatens to overwhelm us—whether it be circumstances, or the attacks of Satan. Friends betrayed him, demons hurled their worst at him, and his enemies nailed him to a cross and disposed of him in a tomb, thinking he was finished with, but on the third day he emerged, victorious. The Christ of today is not a weak, emaciated Christ. He is no longer helplessly nailed to a crucifix. He is a virile, victorious, and valiant Christ.

Illustration

Hudson Taylor summed it up like this: "We are a supernatural people, born again by a supernatural birth; we wage a supernatural fight and are taught by a supernatural teacher, led by a supernatural captain to assured victory."[3]

C. His Message of Victory

"It is I; be not afraid" (6:20). It is a message which *quiets our fears.* The storms are blowing around us, the wind hurling past our rigging, and we feel as if we cannot go any further. Then the Christ of victory appears and says, "Be not afraid." It is a message which *quickens our faith*—"It is I," said the master. His presence makes all the difference and faith finds its anchorage in him.

Illustration

It is reported that the newspaper counselor, Ann Landers, receives an average of 10,000 letters each month, and nearly all of them from people burdened with problems. She was asked if there was any one problem which predominates throughout the letters she receives, and her reply was the one problem above all others seems to be fear. People are afraid of losing their health, their wealth, their loved ones. People are afraid of life itself.[4] How wonderful to know that into this kind of situation Jesus brings a message of victory, "It is I; be not afraid" (6:20).

III. The Christ of Destiny

"Then they willingly received him into the ship: and immediately the ship was at the land whither they went"

(6:21). International leaders may have a lot to say about our world today but in the last analysis the destiny of the nations, and of individuals, is in the hands of one—and only one—the Christ of today. Presently he is going to appear and wrap up this aspect of world history in order to introduce the next drama of his redemptive purpose. Until that moment he waits, as the Christ of victory and of destiny, to be received into our individual hearts and lives.

A. He Assures Progress

"Immediately the ship was at the land" (6:21). Nine hours they had been rowing and had only gone three miles, and were struggling in the center of the lake, like many of our lives—going around in circles, getting nowhere. So many people imagine that through their own reading and studying they can plumb the great mysteries of life. They dip into philosophy, psychology, and other fields of knowledge, but seem to get nowhere. Only when they turn to the Lord Jesus Christ and put their faith in him do they realize a true sense of destiny.

There is nothing more pathetic than an aimless person. As someone has said, "Any dead fish can go with the stream. It takes a live one to swim against it." The Christ of destiny assures us of progress in our life.

Illustration

Stephen Olford recounts an occasion when he was traveling by air from one city to another. He saw a man reading a book titled *A Round Trip to Nowhere.* When the opportunity came, he engaged the man in conversation about eternal issues and was able to share the gospel of Christ who can tell us where we have come from, where we are, and where we are going.

B. He Assures Purpose

"Immediately the ship was at the land *whither they went*" (6:21). It was at Jesus' command that they had set out to reach Capernaum. And God has a plan for every life. There is design in all that he creates. But we fail to achieve his purpose for our lives until we receive Christ. The moment the master was received into the ship there was progress, and soon after, the purpose of the voyage was realized.

Paul sets forth the life of purpose when he writes: "We are his workmanship, created in Christ Jesus unto good works, which God hath before ordained that we should walk in them" (Eph. 2:10). As Christians, we are not here by accident or chance. God has foreordained the path that we should walk. It is our privilege to find, follow, and finish the course that is laid out before us. For the believer, there is not only progress in the Christian life, but also purpose.

Conclusion

In this beautiful little story we have learned three things: that the Christ of today is the Christ of sympathy, who from his vantage point in heaven intercedes and intervenes. We have learned that he is the Christ of victory, coming at just the right moment with just the right message: "It is I; be not afraid" (6:20). And we have learned that he is the Christ of destiny: when he comes in, there is progress and purpose.

Will you do what the disciples did that day? They "willingly [or eagerly] received him into the ship" (6:21). If you do, he says, "I will come in" (Rev. 3:20). Will you ask him in now?

13

The Opening of a Blind Man's Eyes: *Darkness to Dawn*

9:1-11, 35-38

Introduction

Of all the handicaps that can curse men and women, blindness must be one of the saddest. Yet there is something infinitely worse than physical blindness: it is spiritual blindness. Indeed, so real and disastrous is this condition that God considered it necessary to send his Son to earth for the express purpose of opening the eyes of the blind and lightening the darkness of men.

I. The Blind Man's Night

"A man which was blind from his birth" (9:1). In a very real sense, here was a man who was sitting in the darkness of a physical night. This had been his condition from birth; he had never seen the light of day.

This story has been providentially preserved in order to teach us the fact of our spiritual night by nature. As Dr. William Temple simply puts it, "The man 'blind from birth' is every man." No matter how youthful, beautiful, intellectual, or charming you may be, you have been born spiritually blind.

A. A Condition of Tragedy

"Jesus . . . *saw* a man which was blind from his birth" (9:1). The word "saw" means "to perceive mentally." In other words, he did not merely give a cursory glance as he passed; he saw something tragic. The disciples only glanced at the poor man and remarked, judgmentally, that he was receiving the due reward of his sins, or at any rate, that of his parents. But Jesus saw that this man in his blindness was a picture of every man who is born into the world, quite apart from personal or parental sins.

Similarly, we have to recognize that the moral blindness of men and women, boys and girls, is not something we can dismiss with an observation, a speculation, an opinion, or even a disagreement. It is a tragic fact.

B. A Condition of Poverty

After his eyes were opened, his neighbors asked, "Is not this he that sat and begged?" (9:8). A fifth of the world's pleasures and treasures were dead to him. How true this is of those who are still in the darkness of a spiritual night. The Bible tells us that "the natural man receiveth not the things of the Spirit of God: for they are foolishness unto him: neither can he know them, because they are spiritually discerned" (1 Cor. 2:14).

Illustration

A gentleman once tried to describe scarlet to a blind man. When he had done so, the blind man pathetically asked, "Is scarlet like the blast of a trumpet?" To the blind man, scarlet was an enigma; he could not discern it, for he was optically incapable.

So it is with spiritual things. Because men are blind to the things of the Spirit they merely dismiss the pleasures and treasures of the Christian life as foolishness, not realizing what they are missing.

II. The Blind Man's Sight

"Now I *see*" (9:25), cried the blind man, after he had encountered the Lord Jesus. But how did it all happen? The simple answer is that it was a miracle, and miracles cannot be explained. This was something that the religious bigots were not able to accept. All that the man could do was to describe *what* had happened and leave the *how* to Christ who had touched his eyes. As far as he was concerned, there was:

A. The Divine Operation

"He answered and said, A man that is called Jesus made clay, and anointed mine eyes, and said unto me, Go to the pool of Siloam, and wash: and I went and washed, and I received sight" (9:11). How simple and yet how profound! Whatever interpretations may be given of this act of the master's, one thing is quite clear: the whole operation was not only real in itself; it was symbolic of an even deeper reality. This is the only recorded occasion on which Jesus took the initiative in restoring sight. This fact makes the symbolic act even more significant: just as Jesus voluntarily mixed his own spittle with the earth and then anointed the eyes of the blind, so he voluntarily came from heaven and entered an earthly body, in order that through the mixing of himself with human clay he might impart life to the dead eyes of men. We read in Hebrews: "Forasmuch . . . as the children are partakers of flesh and blood, he also himself likewise took part of the same; that through death he might destroy him that had the power of death, that is, the devil" (Heb. 2:14). This was the divine operation which Jesus performed, in order that we might be delivered from the blinding power of the devil.

Amplification

It is said that saliva in the East represents a man's essential nature or being. To use one's spittle in healing suggested profound sympathy.[1]

B. The Human Application

"I went and washed, and I received sight" (9:11), said the man who had been blind. Having anointed him with the clay, the Lord Jesus had told him to go to the pool of Siloam and wash.

Once again, the act is symbolic. The pool of Siloam, which John carefully tells us means "sent," was a specially provided pool of water for ceremonial drinking and cleansing. Jesus had already likened himself to these very waters, when he cried out on the last day of the Feast of Tabernacles, "If any man thirst, let him come unto me, and drink" (John 7:37). So the blind man went, washed, and received his sight. He accepted the divine operation, and then effected the human application, and forthwith he could see!

Similarly, if you would have light in your darkness, and sight for your blindness, you must accept the divine operation. You must believe that when Jesus died at the cross, he finally and completely handled the problem of spiritual blindness. Then, having accepted the divine operation in simple faith, you must effect the human application by taking the cure for blindness which Jesus makes available through his risen life.

Illustration

One of the miracles of modern surgery is the cornea-grafting operation which now gives sight to hundreds of blind people every year.

On Saturday, January 27, 1951, the *Daily Graphic* reported the thrilling story of one such person who received his sight. The man was Hendrik Botha, a thirty-year-old former clerk, who had been blind for ten years. At the expense of a little church in South Africa, he was sent to the famous Manhattan Eye Hospital. The day he arrived in New York a man died in Michigan. At 2:00 A.M. next morning the surgeon removed the cornea of the blind man's right eye and grafted in the replacement from the dead man. It was a success. Later that year a similar operation restored the sight of the left eye. With joy and thanksgiving that knew no bounds, the South African started back home to look for the first time upon a devoted wife and two small daughters. The startling headlines to this remarkable story carried these words: "He will see family through the eyes of a dead man!"

That is the gospel of spiritual sight. Jesus is not only the divine Surgeon, but also the one who has given his life that others might see. He has completed the operation, but you must effect that application by coming to him and receiving the sight which he makes available through his sacrificial life.

III. The Blind Man's Light

"I am the light of the world," Jesus said (9:5). No doubt this man had heard him and had wondered what that meant; but now he knew. He had passed from *darkness to dawn*. He now possessed:

A. *The Light of Positive Certainty*

"One thing I know, that, whereas I was blind, now I see" (9:25). How this man's eyes must have sparkled with joyous confidence, as he affirmed those words of certainty, "One thing I know." It is hard to argue with a man who refuses to budge from the facts of the case. He could not yet give an explanation of the character of the one who had opened his eyes; neither could he enter into the theological and philosophical arguments of those unbelieving Pharisees; but of one thing he was certain: a man called Jesus had opened his blind eyes.

Christianity is propagated by testimony rather than argument. Controversy of which some are very fond, has done little for the cause of Christ, but testimony has done a great deal.

Illustration

Dr. S. D. Gordon tells of a Christian woman whose age began to tell on her memory. She had once known much of the Bible by heart. Eventually only one precious bit stayed with her. "I know whom I have believed, and am persuaded that he is able to keep that which I committed unto him against that day." By and by part of that slipped its hold, and she would quietly repeat, "That which I have committed unto him." At last, as she hovered on the borderline between this and the spirit world, her loved ones noticed her lips moving. They bent down and heard her repeating over and over again to herself the one word of the text, "Him, Him, Him." She had lost the whole Bible, but one word. But she had the whole Bible in that one word.[2]

B. The Light of Patient Constancy

"They reviled him" (9:28). "They cast him out" (9:34). No one can claim the light of certainty without at once encountering unbelieving and bigoted enemies. So we read that his parents, friends, and leaders cold-shouldered him and finally excommunicated him. To a Jew, such treatment constituted the greatest possible shame and ignominy. But in spite of it all, he remained constant and unshaken. In fact, he turned the very persecutions and accusations of his enemies into a most impressive and challenging witness to the Lord Jesus.

So often people say that they would be Christians if only they were assured of the courage and power not to fail when the going was hard. To such people this blind man has a complete answer. His is the light of patient constancy. It shines even when the clouds over-head are dark.

Illustration

Pliny, Roman governor in Asia Minor in the early second century, was so puzzled about the Christians brought before him for trial that he wrote his famous letter to the Emperor Trajan asking for his advice. This was the kind of thing he found himself up against:

A certain unknown Christian was brought before him, and Pliny, finding little fault in him, proceeded to threaten him. "I will banish thee," he said.

"Thou canst not," was the reply, "for all the world is my Father's house."

"Then I will slay thee," said the Governor.

"Thou canst not," answered the Christian, "for my life is hid with Christ in God."

"I will take away thy possessions," continued Pliny.

"Thou canst not, for my treasure is in heaven."

"I will drive thee away from man and thou shalt have no friend left," was the final threat. And the calm reply once more was, "Thou canst not, for I have an unseen Friend from whom thou art not able to separate me." What was a poor, harassed Roman governor, with all the powers of life and death, torture and the stake at his disposal, to do with people like that?[3]

C. The Light of Progressive Clarity

"Now I see" (9:25). It is thrilling to read through the story and see how the light of perception and discernment grows brighter and brighter, as the blind man has strength to receive it. To start with, the Lord Jesus was "a man that is called Jesus" (9:11). Then the blind man declared that he was "a prophet" (9:17). Later he spoke of Christ as a "man . . . of God" (9:33). Finally, he reached that moving climax when he met the Savior face to face and cried, "Lord, I believe," and worshiped him (9:38).

Eye specialists tell us that after certain operations

have been performed on the eyes, it is the procedure to bandage the eyes heavily, and then remove one bandage at a time, as the eyes gain the strength for increased light. In a similar way, God leads all those who come to him for spiritual sight. As they can take it, so he increases the light of clarity.

"But suppose I do not confess my blindness in sin?" you ask. The answer is that such an attitude is fatal. Jesus said, "For judgment I am come into this world, that they which see not [that is, they who own their blindness] might see; and that they which see [or refuse to own their blindness] might be made blind" (9:39). What serious words! May the Lord Jesus never have to say to you what he addressed to those unbelieving and proud Pharisees: "Ye say, We see; therefore your sin remaineth" (9:41).

Conclusion

To say that you *see,* when you are in spiritual darkness, is to seal your doom in sin. God save you from such an end! Rather, may you come to Christ now and take advantage of his divine operation, and then seek the human application of the spiritual sight and light that he alone can give. So will your *darkness* be turned to *dawn,* and your testimony will be:

> Once I was blind, but now I can see;
> The Light of the world is Jesus.

> Philip P. Bliss

14

The Raising to Life of Lazarus: *The Destroyer of Death*
John 11:1–44

Introduction

John records several miracles before the crucifixion, and all are deeply significant. The raising of Lazarus is the last and greatest, for in this sign Jesus reveals himself as the destroyer of death, mankind's last and greatest enemy. If miracles are enacted parables, then the one before us is a magnificent demonstration of Christ's power to bring to life those who are dead in trespasses and sins.

I. Christ Confronts Death

"Our friend Lazarus sleepeth; but I go, that I may awake him out of sleep" (11:11). Scholars tell us that the

Talmud often speaks of a rabbi's death as "sleep" (see Matt. 9:24; 1 Thess. 4:14). Homer refers to death and sleep as "twin sisters." Christ's conscious power to awaken Lazarus from sleep brings new meaning to these ancient concepts, for the Savior came into the world to abolish death. We see, then, that Jesus confronted death in a twofold manner:

A. He Viewed Death Redemptively

"This sickness is not unto death, but for the glory of God, that the Son of God might be glorified thereby" (11:4). Though Jesus knew that Lazarus was going to die, in his plan of redemption death was already conquered. There is only one in the universe who can view death like that. He looks at your life and sees the marks that death has made on you already, for men and women who are "dead in trespasses and sins" (Eph. 2:10) are in the process of perishing. But Christ knows that by virtue of his redemption a mighty, saving work can be effected in the sinner who truly believes.

B. He Viewed Death Realistically

"Our friend Lazarus sleepeth. . . . Lazarus is dead" (11:11, 14). Christ spoke of death as *undisturbed slumber*. He said, "Our friend Lazarus sleepeth" (11:11). Here is a sleep from which there is no awaking, unless the Lord Jesus himself intervenes, and what is true physically is even more true spiritually. This man had ears, but he could not hear; eyes, but he could not see; a heart, but he could not love; a will, but he could not act. And unless Jesus Christ awakens the sinner he will continue to sleep undisturbed. No other voice can awaken; no ingenious invention of philosophers, scientists or educators can ever quicken a dead spirit to life. David the psalmist showed his horror of this perpetual sleep when he cried, "Consider and hear me, O LORD my God: lighten mine eyes, lest I sleep the sleep of death" (Ps. 13:3).

Jesus also spoke of death as *unrelieved separation*—"Lazarus is dead" (11:14). Interpreting this in the light of the New Testament, we understand that "the body without the spirit is dead" (James 2:26). Only God can call back a departed spirit. All manner of claims have been made concerning resurrection, but there is no resurrection without divine intervention. This physical fact has its spiritual counterpart; only God can quicken a dead spirit to life. This is what the apostle means when he says, "And you He has made alive, who were dead in trespasses and sins"; and again: "God, who is rich in mercy, because of His great love with which He loved us, even when we were dead in trespasses, has made us alive together with Christ (by grace you have been saved)" (Eph. 2:1, 4–5, NKJV).

Illustration

Stephen Olford recounts the conversion of a young man who later spent four years in Italy as a missionary. In a subsequent conversation with him, the young man, Jack Kreider, looking back to his conversion, said, "I never cease to wonder at the miracle that took place. It was a Good Friday noon service, and I was brought to church by my aunt. Without any religious background, I was totally dead to spiritual things. As I listened to the message of the cross something happened which instantly changed me from a dead man to a live man in Christ Jesus. I did not even need counseling. I just knew that I was spiritually alive from the dead. The proof of it is that I have gone on to finish college and seminary and am now serving my Lord in the land of Italy. There I have seen those 'dead in trespasses and sins' come to life, even as I was quickened by the Spirit of God."

II. Christ Condemns Death

"When Jesus therefore saw her weeping, and the Jews also weeping which came with her, he groaned in the spirit, and was troubled [or 'was moved with indignation']" (11:33). The reactions of our Lord Jesus in the presence of death are highly significant. The language employed highlights such emotions as agitation and indignation. The narrative demonstrates:

A. The Depth of His Displeasure

"He groaned in the spirit, and was troubled" (11:33). In the Greek, this constitutes "an incongruous combination." As A. T. Robertson puts it: "The word means 'to snort with anger like a horse.' It occurs in the LXX (Dan. 11:30) for violent displeasure. The notion of indignation is present in the other examples of the word in the New Testament (Mark 1:43; 14:5; Matt. 9:30). . . . The presence of these Jews, the grief of Mary, Christ's own concern, the problem of the raising of Lazarus—all greatly agitated the spirit of Jesus. . . . He struggled for self-control."[1] It is my conviction that what moved the Savior to such indignation was the root cause of death, namely, *sin.* "When lust hath conceived, it bringeth forth sin; and sin, when it is finished, bringeth forth death" (James 1:15). "The wages of sin is death; but the gift of God is eternal life through Jesus Christ our Lord" (Rom. 6:23). Death is the inevitable outcome of sin, and one cannot help feeling that with a backward glance through history the Lord Jesus gathered up in a moment the whole tragic story of man's sin. "Wherefore, as by one man sin entered into the world, and death by sin; and so death passed upon all men, for that all have sinned." (Rom. 5:12).

Amplification

S. D. Gordon says that there are seven simple facts that everyone ought to know about sin: The first is that "sin earns wages." The second, "sin pays wages." The third, "sin insists on paying." You may be quite willing to let the account go, but sin always insists on paying. Fourth, "sin pays its wages in kind." Sin against the body brings results in the body. Sin in the mental life brings results there. Sin in contact with other people brings a chain of results affecting those others. It is terribly true that 'no man sinneth to himself.' Sin is the most selfish of acts. It influences to some extent everyone whom we touch. Fifth, "sin pays in installments." Sixth, "sin pays in full, unless the blood of Jesus washes away the stain." Seventh, "sin is self-executive, it pays its own bills. Sin has bound up in itself all the terrific consequences that ever come. . . . The logical result of sin is death; death to the body, death to the mind, death to the soul!" [2]

B. The Depth of His Distress

"Jesus wept" (11:35). Those tears that trickled down his face were not only his expression of oneness and sympathy with Mary and Martha; he was weeping over the damage which sin had brought about. Here was yet another victim of death's relentless hand. All the sin, sorrow and suffering of the world seemed focused within his spirit at that moment. His soul's outburst of grief condemned sin and death.

Illustration

One who knew [George] Whitefield well, and attended his preaching more frequently, perhaps, than any other person, said he hardly ever knew him go through a sermon without weeping; his voice was often interrupted by his tears, which sometimes were so excessive as to stop him from proceeding for a few moments. "You blame me for weeping," he would say, "but how can I help it when you will not weep for yourselves, though your immortal souls are on the verge of destruction, and for ought you know, you are hearing your last sermon, and may never more have an opportunity to have Christ offered to you?"[3]

III. Christ Conquers Death

"I am the resurrection, and the life: he that believeth in me, though he were dead, yet shall he live: and whosoever liveth and believeth in me shall never die" (11:25–26). These words must have startled Martha, for Jesus was not expounding mere doctrine about future events, but rather exposing present realities. He was the resurrection and the life. With those words of triumph he approached the tomb of Lazarus with a fourfold word:

A. *The Word of Preparation*

"Take ye away the stone" (11:39). It would have been the easiest thing in the world for the Lord Jesus to have performed a triple miracle here. He could have rolled away the stone with a word, called Lazarus to life and commanded him to appear with a word. But he did not do so. Instead, he employed those who were standing around to prepare the way. And before he will call to life those who are "dead in trespasses and sins" (Eph. 2:1) he calls on us who are alive spiritually to "roll away the stone."

B. *The Word of Intercession*

"Jesus lifted up his eyes, and said, Father, I thank thee that thou hast heard me" (11:41). Jesus was never out of touch with heaven; and he is demonstrating here his close working relationship with his Father. As A. T. Robertson points out, "Clearly Jesus had prayed to the Father concerning the raising of Lazarus. He has the answer before he acts. 'No pomp of incantation, no wrestling in prayer even; but simple words of thanksgiving, as if already Lazarus was restored' (Dods). Jesus well knew the issues involved on this occasion. If he failed, his own claims to be the Son of God (the Messiah), would be hopelessly discredited with all. If he succeeded, the rulers would be so embittered as to compass his own death."[4]

Archbishop Trench says, "Prayer is not overcoming God's reluctance, it is laying hold of his highest willingness."

C. The Word of Resurrection

"Lazarus, come forth" (11:43). He called out strongly with the word of authority, the voice of the Son of God. "It is just as well he named Lazarus," said an old puritan, "or the whole graveyard would have turned out!" Show me an audience in which the preparation has been done, and a preacher who is in touch with heaven, and I will show you a context in which the word of resurrection brings men and women to life.

Illustration

Dr. A. T. Schofield tells of an occasion when, crossing the English Channel by boat, he heard the loud voice of a small, dirty-looking boy standing near the engine-room. Though Schofield could not hear what was said, he could feel the great paddle wheels slowing down. Again the clear tones were heard, and suddenly the motion of the engines was reversed and the paddles began to turn in an opposite direction. At first it appeared as if the boy had taken control of the vessel. The orders he gave were with authority and the utmost confidence. On getting closer to him the mystery was explained. His eyes were intently fixed on the bridge overhead where the captain stood, giving the orders. He seldom spoke, and then but a word, and yet the boy kept shouting down below as if moved by some unseen power. At last Schofield realized the captain was giving his orders by short, sharp movements of the hand. Unintelligible as they were to the passengers, to the boy every movement had its meaning, and the mighty engines moved in obedience. Pondering this incident, Schofield added: "We wished we were more like the captain's boy. The boy was (like John the Baptist of old) simply 'a voice,' but as the Baptist's voice derived all its importance because it was the Lord's, so did the boy's because it was but an echo of the captain's." In a similar way, Jesus could say, "The Son can do nothing of himself, but what he seeth the Father do: for what things soever he doeth, these also doeth the Son likewise" (John 5:19).[5]

D. The Word of Liberation

"Loose him, and let him go" (11:44). What a startling sight—a man stumbling out of the grave! The heart had started again, the arteries had begun to pulse, and the muscles to operate. So he shuffled out of the tomb, bound hand and foot. That he came out was almost as great a miracle as that he was called to life.

Some of you have been called to life and can remember the day you were converted. But what about the graveclothes that still hamper you—those relics of your past life? You cannot see properly because there is a napkin around your eyes, you cannot work efficiently because your hands are bound. You cannot walk well because the graveclothes still bind your feet. Jesus' word to you is: "Be loosed!"

Observe the three things that proved that Lazarus was alive. There was *communion*—"Lazarus was one of them that sat at the table with him" (John 12:2). Here is a beautiful picture: Mary at Jesus' feet, Martha serving, and Lazarus sitting at table with him. One of the evidences that a person is quickened to life is a worshipping heart, whether in private devotions or at the table of communion. There was *commotion*—"The chief priests consulted that they might put Lazarus also to death" (John 12:10). Where there is spiritual life there is commotion and conflict. It happened in the early church, and throughout the centuries. Jesus told his disciples it would be so (see Matt. 5:11–12; John 15:20). There was *confession*—"By reason of him many of the Jews went away, and believed on Jesus" (John 12:11). One look at Lazarus and they had to believe in Jesus. Here was a man alive from the dead! The evidence of omnipotence is irresistible. The Jews were always seeking after a sign—and here was one in living color. What convinced these unbelievers was not so much what Lazarus had to say, but rather what he was: a man alive from the dead.

Illustration

Many years ago when the great missionary Adoniram Judson was home on furlough, he passed through the city of Stonington, Connecticut. A young boy playing about the wharves at the time of Judson's arrival was struck by the man's appearance. Never before had he seen such a light on any human face. He ran up the street to a minister to ask if he knew who the stranger was. The minister hurried back with him, but became so absorbed in conversation with Judson that he forgot all about the impatient youngster standing near him. Many years afterward that boy . . . became the famous preacher Henry Clay Trumbull. In a book of memoirs he penned a chapter entitled: "What a Boy Saw in the Face of Adoniram Judson." That lighted countenance had changed his life.[6]

Conclusion

The central message of this remarkable miracle is: Jesus the destroyer of death—confronting death redemptively and realistically; condemning death by the depth of his displeasure and distress; and conquering death by the words of preparation, intercession, resurrection and liberation. Throughout the centuries the words still sound: "The dead shall hear the voice of the Son of God: and they that hear shall live" (John 5:25). Will you respond to that voice now?

Endnotes

Introduction

1. John R. W. Stott, "Paralyzed Speakers and Hearers," *Christianity Today* (Mar. 13, 1981), pp. 44–45.

Chapter 1

1. Constance Barnett, quoted in A. Naismith, *1,200 Notes, Quotes and Anecdotes* (Marshall Pickering, an imprint of HarperCollins Publishers), p. 176.
2. Quoted in ibid., p. 73.
3. *The New Scofield Reference Bible* (New York: Oxford University Press, 1967), pp. 128–29. See also Stephen F. Olford, *The Tabernacle: Camping with God* (Neptune, N.J.: Loizeaux Brothers, 1971).
4. Paul Lee Tan, *Encyclopedia of 7,700 Illustrations* (Dallas: Bible Communications, 1979), p. 170.
5. David Livingstone, quoted in ibid., p. 1611.
6. Naismith, *1,200 Notes, Quotes and Anecdotes*, p. 211.
7. Ibid., p. 198.
8. Tan, *Encyclopedia of 7,700 Illustrations*, p. 750.

Chapter 2

1. David L. Currents, quoted in Paul Lee Tan, *Encyclopedia of 7,700 Illustrations* (Dallas: Bible Communications, 1979), p. 503.
2. A. Naismith, *1,200 Notes, Quotes and Anecdotes* (Marshall Pickering, an imprint of HarperCollins Publishers), p. 120.

Chapter 3

1. A. Naismith, *1,200 Notes, Quotes and Anecdotes* (Marshall Pickering, an imprint of HarperCollins Publishers), p. 108.
2. Ibid., p. 49.
3. *Evangelical International High School Quarterly,* quoted in Walter B. Knight, *Knight's Master Book of New Illustrations* (Grand Rapids: Eerdmans, 1956), pp. 235-36.

Chapter 4

1. Paul Lee Tan, *Encyclopedia of 7,700 Illustrations* (Dallas: Bible Communications, 1979), p. 496.
2. Ibid., p. 498.
3. A. Naismith, *1,200 Notes, Quotes and Anecdotes* (Marshall Pickering, an imprint of HarperCollins Publishers), p. 181.
4. The *Ryrie Study Bible* (Chicago: Moody Press, 1978), p. 1620.

Chapter 5

1. A. Naismith, *1,200 Notes, Quotes and Anecdotes* (Marshall Pickering, an imprint of HarperCollins Publishers), p. 53.
2. *Gospel Trumpet,* quoted in Walter B. Knight, *Knight's Master Book of New Illustrations* (Grand Rapids: Eerdmans, 1956), p. 566.
3. Quoted in ibid., p. 562.

Chapter 6

1. *Zion's Herald,* quoted in Walter B. Knight, *3,000 Illustrations for Christian Service* (Grand Rapids: Eerdmans, 1952), p. 584.
2. Marvin R. Vincent, *Word Studies in the New Testament* (Grand Rapids: Eerdmans, 1957), p. 241.
3. *Adventures With God,* quoted in Paul Lee Tan, *Encyclopedia of 7,700 Illustrations* (Dallas: Bible Communications, 1979), pp. 186-87.
4. *The Australian Baptist,* quoted in ibid., p. 737.

Chapter 7

1. Foster, quoted in Paul Lee Tan, *Encyclopedia of 7,700 Illustrations* (Dallas: Bible Communications, 1979), p. 648.

2. A. Naismith, *1,200 Notes, Quotes and Anecdotes* (Marshall Pickering, an imprint of HarperCollins Publishers), p. 29.

3. *The Ryrie Study Bible* (Chicago: Moody Press, 1978), p. 1630.

4. Naismith, *1,200 Notes, Quotes and Anecdotes,* p. 55.

5. Tan, *Encyclopedia of 7,700 Illustrations,* p. 1316.

Chapter 8

1. Aquilla Webb, *1001 Illustrations for Pulpit and Platform* (New York: Harper & Brothers, 1926), p. 96.

2. Daniel Webster, quoted in Paul Lee Tan, *Encyclopedia of 7,700 Illustrations* (Dallas: Bible Communications, 1979), p. 373.

3. *The Ryrie Study Bible* (Chicago: Moody Press, 1978), p. 1603.

4. Walter B. Knight, *3,000 Illustrations for Christian Service* (Grand Rapids: Eerdmans, 1952), p. 438.

5. A. Naismith, *1,200 Notes, Quotes and Anecdotes* (Marshall Pickering, an imprint of HarperCollins Publishers), pp. 44-45.

Chapter 9

1. A. Naismith, *1,200 Notes, Quotes and Anecdotes* (Marshall Pickering, an imprint of HarperCollins Publishers), p. 66.

2. *Now,* quoted in Walter B. Knight, *3,000 Illustrations for Christian Service* (Grand Rapids: Eerdmans, 1952), p. 471.

3. Burrell, *Christ and Progress,* quoted in ibid., p. 251.

4. Quoted in ibid., p. 248.

Chapter 10

1. *Pastor's Manual,* quoted in Paul Lee Tan, *Encyclopedia of 7,700 Illustrations* (Dallas: Bible Communications, 1979), pp. 1284-85.

2. Willis Cook, quoted in ibid., p. 1284.

3. *The Upper Room,* quoted in Walter B. Knight, *3,000 Illustrations for Christian Service* (Grand Rapids: Eerdmans, 1952), p. 250.

4. *Youth for Christ Magazine,* quoted in A. Naismith, *1,200 Notes, Quotes and Anecdotes* (Marshall Pickering, an imprint of HarperCollins Publishers), p. 204.

5. *Earnest Worker,* quoted in Walter B. Knight, *Knight's Master Book of New Illustrations* (Grand Rapids: Eerdmans, 1956), p. 18.

6. *Sunday School Times,* quoted in ibid., p. 716.

7. G. Franklin Allee, *Evangelistic Illustrations for Pulpit and Platform* (Chicago: Moody Press, 1961), p. 243.

Chapter 11

1. C. H. Spurgeon, quoted in Walter B. Knight, *3,000 Illustrations for Christian Service* (Grand Rapids: Eerdmans, 1952), p. 372.

2. Paul Lee Tan, *Encyclopedia of 7,700 Illustrations* (Dallas: Bible Communications, 1979), p 1075.

3. Al Bryant, quoted in ibid., p. 496.

4. Quoted in ibid., p. 1081.

5. Ibid., p. 504

6. G. Franklin Allee, *Evangelistic Illustrations for Pulpit and Platform* (Chicago: Moody Press, 1961), p. 162.

Chapter 12

1. A. Naismith, *1,200 Notes, Quotes and Anecdotes* (Marshall Pickering, an imprint of HarperCollins Publishers), p. 155.

2. Paul Lee Tan, *Encyclopedia of 7,700 Illustrations* (Dallas: Bible Communications, 1979), p. 504.

3. Walter B. Knight, *Knight's Master Book of New Illustrations* (Grand Rapids: Eerdmans, 1956), p. 716.

4. *The Bible Friend,* quoted in Tan, *Encyclopedia of 7,700 Illustrations,* p. 434.

Chapter 13

1. A. Naismith, *1,200 Notes, Quotes and Anecdotes* (Marshall Pickering, an imprint of HarperCollins Publishers), p. 187.

2. *American Holiness Journal,* quoted in Paul Lee Tan, *Encyclopedia of 7,700 Illustrations* (Dallas: Bible Communications, 1979), p. 239.

3. Quoted in ibid., p. 993.

Chapter 14

1. A. T. Robertson, *Word Pictures in the New Testament,* vol. 5 (Nashville: Broadman Press, 1960, renewed 1988), p. 202.

2. *Earnest Worker,* from Walter B. Knight, *3,000 Illustrations for Christian Service* (Grand Rapids: Eerdmans, 1952).

3. Paul Lee Tan, *Encyclopedia of 7,700 Illustrations* (Dallas: Bible Communications, 1979).

4. A. T. Robertson, *Word Pictures,* p. 205.

5. A. Naismith, *1,200 Notes, Quotes and Anecdotes* (Marshall Pickering, an imprint of HarperCollins Publishers), adapted.

6. Tan, *Encyclopedia of 7,700 Illustrations.*

For Further Reading

Part 1: God Alive in Discourses from the Gospel of John

Barclay, William. *Daily Study Bible* (John). Rev. ed. Philadelphia: Westminster Press, 1975–1976.

Ironside, H. A. *Addresses on the Gospel of John.* Neptune, N.J.: Loizeaux Brothers, Inc., 1942.

Morgan, G. Campbell. *The Gospel According to John.* Westwood, N.J.: Fleming H. Revell Co., 1933.

Tasker, R. V. G. *The Gospel According to St. John.* Tyndale New Testament Commentaries. Grand Rapids: Wm. B. Eerdmans Publishing Co., 1960.

Tenney, Merrill C. *John: The Gospel of Belief.* Grand Rapids: Wm. B. Eerdmans Publishing Co., 1948.

Westcott, B. F. *The Gospel According to St. John.* Grand Rapids: Wm. B. Eerdmans Publishing Co., 1950.

Part 2: God Alive in Miracles from the Gospel of John

Bruce, Alexander Balmain. *The Miracles of Christ.* Minneapolis: Klock and Klock Christian Publishers, 1980.

Hendriksen, William. *A Commentary on the Gospel of John.* 2 vols. New Testament Commentary. Grand Rapids: Baker Book House, 1953.

Laidlaw, John. *Studies in the Miracles of Our Lord.* Minneapolis: Klock and Klock Christian Publishers, 1982.

Lewis, C. S. *Miracles: A Preliminary Study.* New York: Macmillan Publishing House, 1947.

Lockyer, Herbert. *All the Miracles of the Bible: The Supernatural in Scripture, Its Scope and Significance.* Grand Rapids: Zondervan Publishing House, 1961.

MacDonald, George. *The Miracles of Our Lord.* Wheaton, Ill.: H. Shaw Publishers, 1980.

Morris, Leon. *Studies in the Fourth Gospel.* Grand Rapids: Wm. B. Eerdmans Publishing Co., 1969.

————. *The Gospel of John.* New International Commentary of the New Testament. Grand Rapids: Wm. B. Eerdmans Publishing Co., 1970.

Pink, Arthur W. *Exposition of the Gospel of John.* Grand Rapids: Zondervan Publishing House, 1975.

Ryrie, Charles Caldwell. *The Miracles of Our Lord.* Nashville: Thomas Nelson Publishers, 1984.

Scroggie, William Graham. *Guide to the Gospels.* London: Pickering & Inglis, 1962.

Spurgeon, Charles H. *Sermons on the Miracles.* Vol. 3. Library of Spurgeon's Sermons, ed. Charles T. Cook. Vol. 3. Grand Rapids: Zondervan Publishing House, 1958.

Taylor, William Mackergo. *Miracles of Our Saviour.* Grand Rapids: Kregel Publications, 1975.

Trench, Richard Chenevix. *Notes on the Miracles of Our Lord.* London: Pickering & Inglis, 1953.